IF BORROWED AT DUBBO, PLEASE
REFER TO PRINTED RECEIPT FOR
DATE DUE.

95
95

95
95

995

6

1997
997

998
1998

DOORWAYS
•A YEAR OF THE•
CUMBERDEEN DIARIES

DOORWAYS

• A YEAR OF THE •

CUMBERDEEN DIARIES

ERIC ROLLS

Photographs by John Peel

ANGUS
& ROBERTSON
PUBLISHERS

For Elaine, who also fashioned this remarkable year

This diary was first published in the Sun-Herald

Angus & Robertson Publishers'
creative writing programme is
assisted by the Australia Council,
the Federal Government's arts
funding and advisory body.

ANGUS & ROBERTSON PUBLISHERS

Unit 4, Eden Park, 31 Waterloo Road,
North Ryde, NSW, Australia 2113;
94 Newton Road, Auckland 1,
New Zealand; and
16 Golden Square, London W1R 4BN,
United Kingdom

First published in Australia
by Angus & Robertson Publishers in 1989
First published in New Zealand
by Angus & Robertson NZ Ltd in 1989

Text copyright © Eric Rolls, 1989

National Library of Australia
Cataloguing-in-publication data

Rolls, Eric, 1923–
    Doorways: a year of the Cumberdeen diaries.
    ISBN 0 207 16200 X.

    1. Rolls, Eric, 1923–   —Diaries. 2. Country
    life—New South Wales—Baradine Region.
    3. Baradine Region N.S.W.—Biography.
    I. Peel, John, 1943–   . II. Title.
994.4'4'00994

Typeset in 11pt Baskerville
by Midland Typesetters, Maryborough, Victoria
Printed in Australia
by Australian Print Group

Introduction

It was a remarkable year. Several dreams crystallised. Five big chapters of a book I had been working on for twenty years, *Flowers and the Wide Sea*, a human history of the Chinese in Australia, had taken shape on hundreds of pages. Words that had been singing in my head since the first days of research were now set in permanent ink. It was possible to write the work, to bring hundreds of books, hundreds of journals and magazines, thousands of photocopies and newspaper clippings, hundreds of thousands of words of notes—an enormous mass of stuff—into exciting and lucid order.

Now it was imperative that I make a last long research trip. It is a poor historian who writes about what he has not seen. His facts have no flesh on them. Soon after I began the work, I planned to go to the Palmer River in north Queensland where 17,000 Chinese dug for gold last century. They established busy towns, big gardens, piggeries; they bred ducks and fowls where it is now as remote and as difficult to approach as it was then. The dry areas of Australia eradicate traces of man as quickly as tropic jungle. And I needed to see the Asian north of the Northern Territory, to drive up into wet unfamiliar country that was familiar to the Chinese who landed at Darwin and walked south to goldfields in the dry unfamiliar. And I wanted to find the ruby fields in central Australia. I did not even know where they were when we left home. There is an especial wonder in indefinite journeys.

I say 'we'. The wondrous loses much of its wonder if one lives it alone. It is too much for a single consciousness. I had been working alone since my wife Joan died, and the writing was going as well as ever, better perhaps. It had to, or else I would negate Joan's life as well as mine. Elaine had come up to sort the Chinese papers, to give me cardboard boxes of stuff that applied to one chapter only so that I did not have to do a month's sorting for each chapter. She brought the old house to life again: hard work, good food, good wine and love. So I said, 'Come with me

. . . a building we call
the old school house

somewhere north. We'll learn where as we go and we'll come home when we've finished.'

We had to buy a lot of equipment, an extra fuel tank for the Landcruiser, a long-distance radio, a refrigerator and another battery to power it, an aluminium canopy to fit the utility tray, an offroad trailer. The costs were frightening and we were wondering how we could get wherever we were going and back without exceeding the overdraft—it seemed impossible—when I received an extraordinary telephone call. The Australia-China Council asked how much of the Chinese book I had written, how much more was there to write, did I have to do any more research, would $10,000 be any use to me?

Elaine wrote to the Australian Heritage Commission. She explained that we would be visiting sites of Chinese life where relics had never been recorded. Here was a chance to get them recorded for a good fee only, there would be no travel expenses. The Commission knew her capabilities, they employed her.

Then Tim Dodd of the *Sun-Herald* rang and asked for the diary. I said yes because that would ensure we would get home in credit, but I expected it to interfere with research and with writing. It did not, it added a remarkable overlay of excitement and pulled more out of both of us. Instead of resting as we moved from one bout of research to the next (we went through the holdings of every library, every historical society in every town we passed through), I was keyed up making notes about what I saw, what Elaine saw. She made me aware of buildings, of the life in vernacular architecture. Single skin wooden walls with the studs exposed were not originally a freak of fashion, they were an economical necessity. The exterior boards were intended to go on when the money was made to pay for them. Then it was realised such houses cooled more quickly as high daytime temperatures fell at night, so builders nailed chamfered weatherboards on the inside of the studs and grooved them so that they looked like narrow lining boards on the interior. I would not have missed the variety of termite mounds, I usually knew what species built them, but I would have missed the individual ventilators that crown the iron roofs of Townsville.

Neither of us expected the beauty of central Australia. We know our own hills and plains under white light, green light, blue light, yellow light, golden. We had not imagined mauve land under pink light, or a light that would not allow hills that are jagged beyond the meaning of the word any suggestion of blue, no matter what the distance. They cut the sky unblurred by Rayleigh scattering.

At first I feared that the length of the articles, 700 to 900 words, would be too restrictive, then I found it a good discipline to work under. It demanded that each piece be constructed as precisely as a poem. The diary begins at the time of sowing crops, it ends at the time of sowing. A farmer's year moves in cycles of sowing, harvest, sowing; of expectation, reality, expectation. A writer's life moves in much the same way. Each ending challenges the next beginning.

Eric Rolls

There are equally lovable
places to live,
but none better

This will not be a day-by-day account, but a response to the vital things of each week. On the land one is always aware of life. Under one's feet the soil grows. It does not lie in one sulky position like a bitumen road.

My farm, Cumberdeen, is north-west of the sawmilling village of Baradine. In the late 1830s and 1840s it was part of a run known as Pretty Plains. There were scattered big trees and many shrubs and flowering plants. But it was open country. No one would have thought of clearing it. The grasses were deep-rooted perennials with millet-like seeds. They too grew in scattered clumps. The soil was spongy. One could rake the top five centimetres through the fingers.

Sheep and cattle hardened the soil. The good grasses died and their inferior cousins with vicious corkscrew seeds took over. During the long drought of the 1870s, soils powdered under too many cloven hoofs. When the rain came and continued, cypress pine and other trees sprang out of the bare ground as they do after fire. The growth drove out men and livestock. Then settlers moved in and cleared it for farming. They were expert judges of soil. Our northern boundary sharply divides deep sandy loam that will grow anything from the difficult acid soil of the Pilliga Forest that grows superb White Cypress Pine timber and Narrow-leaf Ironbark, but little else of monetary worth.

So once again we have pretty plains, farmland dotted with Kurrajong, Wilga, White Cypress Pine, an occasional Whitewood or Rosewood, and clumps and green roads of several species of box and many shrubs. To the south we look at the Warrumbungle Mountains, some days blue, distant and hazy, some days green and so near we can see individual trees. We are sandwiched between mountains and forests. There are equally lovable places to live, but none better.

For most of this week the mountains have been retouched with white. The new lines showed up whenever the snow clouds lifted. We saw them first from the sheep yards. We had run the ewes in to mark the last batch of lambs, but a day that had promised to grow warmer grew suddenly colder and we decided not to mark them. On a good day the lambs seem little aware of drawn testicles and tails squirting blood. They run to their mothers, have a consolatory drink, then move out to eat pasture as though nothing much has happened. But extreme weather on top of what is usually minor discomfort might throw them into shock.

While we were mustering the ewes we came on an abandoned lamb. It had been dropped early in the night and was nearly frozen. Elaine, who has been working for me as literary assistant and who joins in everything that I do, picked it up and warmed it under her jumper. In the yards we found its mother and stronger twin. Only half-a-dozen lambs had been dropped during the night and it was not hard to find the lamb that matched it. I caught the mother and we gave the lamb a good drink of colostrum. But it was still very weak and the mother showed no interest in it at all.

I considered whether it was worth the effort of penning the ewe for a week until she changed her mind. Undecided and unenthusiastic I stalled while I ran the mob into a bigger yard and made a count of those ready for market, always a pleasant job when the prices are high. Then Elaine noticed that one of the ewes that had just raced through the gate stopped and dropped a lamb. She took over the stray, smeared it all over with birth slime, and left the mother licking them both.

Elaine had seen European snow out of plane windows but had never seen it close. We took the four-wheel drive up into the Warrumbungles. Big saplings of Mountain Hickory, Red Gum and Rough-barked Apple wore snow in their crevices as self-consciously as confetti. Only those Australian

To the south we look
at the Warrumbungle Mountains . . .

trees that grow above the common snowline are shaped to deal with snow. The others are V-shaped to channel rain down their branches, down their trunks to surface roots. They collect snow in odd little blobs. All snow on the ground had melted, but logs bore it as brilliantly as new paint.

Before I went to bed I drove up to check on the ewe we had imposed on. She had stayed in the big yard and both lambs were on their feet drinking from her. It was almost snowing. The flakes were melting high in the air and drifting down as flakes of rain.

*Townsmen have no idea
of the authority of the weather.
It oversees our lives . . .*

It is raining again, hours of steady, light rain occasionally shaken down harder by a crack of thunder. Unexpected, unforecast, it was just in time for crops and pasture growing on a minimum of moisture. But it caught us with sheep in the yards overnight. Elaine and I had been drafting off those that need only a polishing up in a good paddock before they are ready for sale and we did not get finished before dark. It was slow work picking out dry ewes from those whose udders were shrivelling after feeding lambs for two to three months. Right hand marked backs with raddle, left hand felt under each ewe.

So I walked in the rain for hours this morning moving two flocks of sheep back to paddocks. A pair of twins and another lamb had been dropped in the muddy yards. They were healthy and full of milk but moved slowly, their mothers turning round and fussing each time they fell a couple of metres behind. I drove to the fast-moving front of the mob and made sure the leaders headed in the right direction, then walked back to bring on the ewes with the youngest lambs at their own speed. Water squelched inside my riding boots. Drops collected on my neck and ran off in cold runnels down my back. The ewe we gave the extra lamb to last week was in the middle of the mob. Her twins can now keep up with her on any drive. One, her own, is small, tight-woolled and wrinkly, the other big, plain-bodied and fluffy. It is possible to get real twins as dissimilar as that. Sometimes they are the progeny of two rams.

This year, for the first time in thirty-eight years, I have no sown crops to appreciate the rain. For thirty-five of those years I worked myself under the obdurate control of the weather. No matter what we had planned for the next week, next month, the rain thudded its own commands on the

The old ewes grew wool, they widened with flesh,
they bloomed with fat

roof: 'Start the tractor, hook up to the plough,' 'Sow the cowpeas,' 'Sow the sunflowers,' 'Sow the barley,' 'Spray the saffron thistles.' Sometimes in the middle of a November night it would rattle down an order: 'Cover the bins! Cover the bins!' And we would leap out of bed, run to the Land Rover with its pile of tarpaulins in the back, and drive to the full bins of grain that we had left uncovered because there had not been a cloud in the sky and there seemed no risk whatever of rain. Townsmen have no idea of the authority of weather. It oversees our lives, our livelihood.

For the last three years I employed a sharefarmer. On my sixtieth birthday I happened to be working out how many years it would take me to write the next five books: say another three years on this one, eighteen months, two years on that, seven years' research and writing on the next big one. Then I realised with considerable shock how old I would be. I decided from then on to work words a day every day instead of acres. But the sharefarmer came from Western Australia where the weather is predictable. He treated it more as a benign friend than a master. He grew some fine crops, but as it seemed to me his friend must eventually turn against him, we parted.

So for much of the last year and all of this year we have been buying cheap, drought-stricken sheep out of the Dubbo saleyards, fattening them up in about four months, selling them all, then buying in again. Something always seems to grow on this place. The first lot of several hundred went into heavy lupin stubble where there was a lot of shelled grain. We paid $1.20 a head for them. They were humpbacked, their shorn skins hung untidily on jagged bones, they had not an incisor tooth in their heads. Bottom gum met top gum. We wondered if they could handle the stiff stubble of lupins, the very hard-shelled grain. In a few days they learnt to pick the white grains up in their lips, work them one by one under their molars, and crack them like nuts before swallowing them. We could hear them feeding from a couple of hundred metres away, dozens of simultaneous little explosions. The old ewes grew wool, they widened with flesh, they bloomed with fat. They went to the abattoirs looking like young sheep. We avoided thinking about where they were going as we loaded them. One never quite learns to regard one's animals with sufficient pragmatism.

We cut . . . anything
that will bend the flames
and vary the pattern

O ur fires supply more than warmth. We watch them, listen to them, smell them. It takes so little extra trouble to build a special fire. Certainly we have advantages. The Forestry Commission in Baradine sells permits that allow us to go out into the forest and collect our own logs.

So we cut Bull Oak that burns with an aromatic smell, and leaves little ash; we cut Budda, that burns like incense and cuts like iron; we cut Bimble Box with a tight circular grain and heavy Narrow-leaf Ironbark as a staple. We cut hollow logs, and pieces with knots or splits, or forked hollows: anything that will bend the flames and vary the pattern.

Twigs bearing dead gum leaves or box leaves mixed in with the kindling cause a crackle of sound and a crackle of smells as they catch. White smoke, grey smoke, black, green and blue smoke puff up from the wood, then all becomes a mass of yellow flame. After a while the different logs burn with their own flames. We see patches of green, orange, red, blue, white, yellow, long and short flame, fat and thin. An orange flame bends into the end of a hollow log. Gas hisses out the other and almost escapes, but inevitably the heat catches it. There is a little pop, and pink tongues of flame lick up the chimney.

Most nights in winter we eat dinner in front of the fire. The setting makes good food especially voluptuous. One night this week we ate a voluptuous steak, one never produced in Australia before, Kobe No. 1 on the fanatical Japanese scale of excellence. The piece that served four of us would

Our fires supply more than warmth

have sold for over \$300 in Japan. We acknowledged it with a sauce made of black olives and true, rich malmsey from Madeira.

The Americans have spent millions trying to produce Kobe steak. Sometimes they have succeeded, but never at a cost that would be economic. What is it? The Japanese have many grades of beef. After the ordinary lines, the six superior grades run from Kobe 0 to Kobe 5. It is beef fattened so that the flesh is marbled with fine, white veins of fat. In Kobe 5 each vein is the same size, no piece of meat bigger than a square centimetre misses veining. The Japanese slice it wafer thin, then layer it on a platter so that the marbling matches. Taking the first slice in the chopsticks is like cracking a fine piece of pink Italian marble. One holds it briefly in boiling stock—it takes no more than a second to cook—then eats it. It melts in the mouth but has little flavour. The Japanese abhor the smell of ordinary meat cooking.

They produce their Kobe steak by feeding cattle in single stalls for up to 300 days. They massage them with straw whisks once a day, they pet them, they reward them for a good day's eating with a bottle of beer.

The steak that we ate was off an Angus steer that had been fed for 115 days only on a complex ration no other cattle have ever eaten. Next to be killed, at 150 days, will be an Angus heifer. Female cattle naturally deposit more intramuscular fat than males. John Rich, my son-in-law, a veterinary scientist specialising in animal nutrition, expects that the heifer will make Kobe No. 4. If she does he will fly with her carcass and several others to Japan. The prospects are exciting.

In conjunction with my daughter, Kerry Jane, a physiotherapist, and his parents, Alan and Daphne Rich, John runs a feed lot that is growing day by day. It houses 1500 cattle and 15,000 sheep at present. The Kobe feeding trial is at the request of a Japanese firm.

The Angus yearlings, already prime before going into the yard, are being fed a ration of twenty per cent fat in the form of palm oil and up to thirty per cent protein in a form devised by a brilliant

CSIRO scientist. It enfolds fat and resists rumen bacteria. So the first three stomachs that depend on bacterial digestion work on the cotton hulls and the chaff and the grain in the ration. The fat and protein pass untouched to the fourth stomach. It would be impossible for bacteria to digest that amount of fat. First the bacteria would die, then the beast. In the fourth stomach gastric acid breaks down the coating and digests protein and fat quickly. The beasts absorb it happily.

No one gives them bottles of beer. But passers-by stop to talk to them. It is difficult to find the right words. Ought one tell them how round they are getting, how pretty their meat will look on a Japanese platter?

*. . . so different a land
it was more a new planet
than a new continent*

During the week John Peel, an outstanding English-born photographer and journalist, called in to see us. He is preparing a book on New South Wales for which eleven authors have each written a chapter, and wanted to add his photographs on the section I wrote on what New South Wales looked like when the white man arrived and how it has changed.

We walked up to a patch of Oat Grass, *Themeda australis*, that grows well in a corner of the farm protected from stock. Purple-stemmed and heavy-headed with oat-like seeds, this lovely grass grew from Hobart to Darwin on the wettest coast and driest inland. Our first stockkeepers, many of them with years of their own experience and with hundreds of years of farming tradition behind them, described it as a fine, fattening grass, equal to any that grew in England. It lasted about six years in most districts. Those first farmers cannot be blamed for not foreseeing that what looked sturdy was delicate. Nothing they knew served them. Australia was so different a land it was more a new planet than a new continent.

The Oat Grass that grows today is still beautiful but it is no longer palatable, no longer nourishing. Phosphorus added to the soil as a chemical and in the concentrated dung of European mammals has coarsened it; nitrogen, supplied by European medics that have run wild, has deepened the green of its leaves and deranged their flavour.

We photographed also a Kurrajong that sprouted in the top of a five-metre-tall dead stump about fifty years ago, a fine example of opportunism. Probably a currawong dropped a seed there. They eat a lot of Kurrajong seeds and also the imported Pepper Tree berries, digest the thin measure of flesh on each, then regurgitate what they do not want in loosely compacted cylinders on fence posts, in stock troughs, in trees, along garden paths. As the sapling grew, its roots travelled down into the ground through the mud guts termites had stuffed the stump with. The stump confined and directed the expanding roots. They spiralled, overlapped, plaited themselves together. Now a thick ten-strand cable has burst the old stump apart and revealed itself. What ought to be hidden underground stands up like a grotesque trunk. A mammal is propped upright on its bowels.

Elaine took John Peel to the Wooleybah sawmill, one of the few mills in Australia still working within the forest it draws its timber from. Modern sawmills have become a town industry. Logs are carted in to them.

Wooleybah cuts the beautiful, aromatic White Cypress Pine. Australia sent samples of this timber to the Colonial and Indian Exhibition held in India in 1886. The judges not only examined it, they sawed it, planed it, nailed it, screwed it and tested it for strength. They pronounced it 'straight-grained, durable, beautifully figured and easy to work'.

Many Australian timbers earned high praise at several international exhibitions last century. Few of them have been appreciated in Australia. White Cypress Pine was regarded as cheap cladding, nailed on walls as horizontal weatherboards and painted. The knots in it rejected paint for years and maintenance became too costly. But erected upright in thick, wide unplaned boards and oiled every year or so it makes a house look as though it is growing beautifully in its landscape, not imposing on it.

As flooring it is magnificent, but now expensive. The planed boards have to be turned upside down, clamped together with levers, nailed down temporarily, then left to season for a month while the rest of the house is built over them. Then they have to be turned, clamped, nailed, and when the heads of the nails have been punched down, sanded, oiled, polished. Such floors seem to be living things. The yellow glow changes with the light, the brown knots eddy. Modern needs have

. . . a thick ten-strand cable
has burst the old stump apart . . .

become more prosaic. Cheap, wide, manufactured solid sheets are stapled down by machine to support the carpet.

In an earlier book by John Peel, where he explores marvellously light on rock and corrugated iron, on water and desert sand, he said his early impression of Australia was of 'a country that felt—and all too often looked—as though it had never been loved'.

Certainly from the first days it has not been understood. Even now drought is regarded as a calamity, rather than a necessity. Special provisions are made by governments for drought as for earthquake and cyclone. Drought is a natural way for our soil to restore itself and all native plants cope with it. Australia does not live by seasons. It lives by fits and starts according to rainfall.

. . . I work better because of the window . . .

*But always our visitors
hope to see animals*

I write with my back to a broad window. The imagination works better against a blank wall. But I work better because of the window nevertheless. The sun comes in so kindly on winter mornings. I can feel it, revel in it, without disordering my thoughts. And during the pauses I allow myself to hear things through the glass.

The pair of Brown Quail that have been with us for years keep in contact with a double-note whistle whenever they feed apart. Twice a year they hatch out eight to ten young ones. Often the whole family feeds under a rosemary bush growing no more than a metre from my chair. They scratch and peck. Plump, oval birds, breasts finely barred with black, they are rare in homestead gardens, rare enough anywhere away from swamps or running water.

A Spotted Bowerbird hides in a Kurrajong and miaows like a cat, barks like a fox, caws like a distant raven, squawks over and over the intolerable insistent feeding demands of young Olive-backed Orioles, then, after a silence, makes bumping noises and scrapings and footsteps and the sound of heavy things settling down onto leafy ground that must surely be the chorus of a sleeper cutter unloading his utility before he begins work.

On summer mornings a Superb Blue Wren cleans up the insects that have stuck in the gauze the night before. Tiny toes make tiny clutching sounds, beak pecks lightly. I turn round sometimes to watch him. No more than sixty centimetres from my shoulder, an exquisitely enamelled living miniature is so engrossed in feeding he is unaware of me. Once when I looked it was not the blue wren there but a male Variegated Wren with a purple saddle instead of royal blue. He was on a brief visit with his several females and unknowingly, or knowingly, usurped a feeding ground.

Our human visitors seldom come to dinner parties or on visits measured in hours, they come to seek information, or to bring it, or to see specific things, and they come to stay till the job is done. We work well, then when we have earned it, we eat well and drink well. But always our visitors hope to see animals.

In drought, at the height of a dry summer, it is easy. I put up hessian and bough hides on forest waters, and, if the visitors are willing to sit still and silent for hours, I can guarantee them marvels. A goanna races from man if it sees him and climbs the nearest big tree, warily spiralling to keep the width of the tree between itself and a circling watcher. It seems a frightened creature. When an old man goanna comes to water naturally he parades himself, aware of the authority of jaws and claws. Forked tongue flicks, assessing the air, head swings as he looks all round. Now and again he stops, raises his body clear of the ground, flies his tail like a pennant. He is two metres of power not even a Dingo would dare to tackle. Galahs shriek and tumble above him. Noisy Miners shrill alarm calls. Only a Willie Wagtail drinks as he drinks. For twenty minutes he controls the one water in a thousand hectares.

In good seasons animals are split on many waters. One can go out day after day and see nothing memorable, which is as it ought to be—wonders are not commonplace. So then I take visitors to the artificial stumps Robert Bustard built in 1962 when he began studying lizards in the Pilliga Forest. He made a hundred of them. Ninety centimetres high and forty-five centimetres in diameter, they're made of wood and flat iron covered with two layers of linoleum spaced three millimetres apart with wooden slats. More perfect homes than nature ever provided.

Half of them are still in good order and four species of geckoes, night lizards, inhabit them, including the big, beautiful Ocellated Velvet Gecko that looks and feels like blue, green and purple fur. One must handle them carefully or they will cast their tails. At first they struggle, then, when they feel the warmth of a hand, they stretch out along it unwilling to leave.

Once, and only once, when I undid a nut and eased back the outer layer, the stump erupted with a species of flat, cinnamon-coloured huntsman spiders, thousands of them. Spider had been resting on spider. They swarmed over the stump, over me, over the ground about me. I kept still till they settled down. It is unlikely they are poisonous and they had no reason to bite anyway.

But what a terror to insects they must have been when they went out to feed each night, so many mouths, so very many legs. It must have seemed to a beetle in their path that the very soil had moved in hunger.

 *All that is left of the house are the ironbark blocks it stood on*

In the old city of Xian in China, the beginning and the end of the Silk Road, where a high street crossed a low street, I walked under a bridge that people had walked under for 800 years. We saw rice growing where farmers grew grain 3000 years ago. At Bath in England, Elaine sat on stones worn smooth by naked Romans 2000 years ago and she dabbled a hand in the hot, sulphurous water they played in.

By one side of our house there is a building we call the old school house. We keep the lawnmower in it. For years it served as the electric light shed with a diesel-powered Lister engine sitting on a cement block and big, glass-walled storage batteries in a line on solid shelves. A yellow-flowered creeper almost covers it, grown so out of hand it has reached across to a nearby Kurrajong and climbed it, and twenty metres of Kurrajong bloom preposterously yellow in November. Branches of the creeper lace under the board ceiling. Spiders and hornets build among them. Where one can see the outside walls, it is plain that they were built of White Cypress Pine milled out of the old greys that no longer exist, timber with few knots and big enough to be milled in wide slabs. They were laid on in the old overlapped fashion. If the walls were the hull of a ship, one would say it was clinker-built. The building seems ancient.

Yet a near neighbour, Harry Hadfield, who called in to see us the other day, told us he went to school there in the 1930s along with several other nearby farmers. Big Miss Hatton and Little Miss Hatton, Nina and Zita, taught them. They worked at one the few jobs easily open to women at that time. Their father and brothers built the school for them. It is only fifty years old and served

A fence that seems part of the past . . .

as the summer school. The homestead shaded it and channelled wind through open doors and windows. A better lined and less draughty building, now two detached bedrooms, was the winter school.

A fence that seems part of the past was in good order then, too. In the 1920s the Hattons, short of money but not of time, fenced off the rabbits from their horse paddock with a paling fence. They split pine palings on the property, stood them up hard against one another and laced them together with soft black wire. The children climbed over them on their way to school. It would have never been successful in keeping back rabbits. They would have simply dug under it. And it was not meant to last or else the Hattons would have spent more energy and split the tough ironbark.

There are tracks along the green roads edging our boundaries cut by bullock wagons hauling logs last century and this century. In the eighteen years I have been here they have grown fainter and young trees are overgrowing them. In one corner of a paddock there is a low, smooth mound next to a hollow, the seeming aged site of the busy pitsaw put down in the 1920s by the miller who exploited the pine that sprang up on these plains in the 1880s.

A few months ago we drove out to see the ruins of a house off Mag's Road in the Pilliga Forest. Mag Morrissey lived there until the 1950s. She cut a few sleepers, bred cockerels to sell in Baradine. The place was alive for me before I got there. A man had told me about having a meal with her. They ate in a room with a wide iron chimney at one end of the table. She cooked him a big steak that she had butchered herself. After the meal, she washed up in a tin dish, then turned, and with a quick twist of her wrists, flung the water up and out the top of the chimney.

The chimney has rusted away, the stones that flanked it on the outside lie in a crumbling heap. All that is left of the house are the ironbark blocks it stood on. One seems to be looking at sixteenth century ruins.

Although our artefacts have not lasted, our mountains have lasted so long they seem ready to crumble into soil. The Warrumbungles look insubstantial. The volcanoes that spurted fire over most of the north-west are little conical hills on the flat Liverpool Plains.

*The abattoir
is especially grim
in the early morning*

The letter was on the kitchen table when we got up: 'Dear father, I called in to borrow a couple of sharp knives. I forgot the key of our office where our equipment is kept and I didn't want to go back home—I got bogged twice on the way out.' My daughter, Kerry Jane, was on her way to the Gunnedah Abattoir, 200 kilometres away, for a 5 a.m. start to QA their chiller full of lambs from the previous day's kill. QA means quality assess. What is really means is quality assurance. Since the scandal of kangaroo meat substitution a few years ago, directors of meat export companies have to guarantee their product.

Kerry Jane is a physiotherapist, a satisfying occupation. 'Look how I can walk,' an excited ex-patient called to her in Coonamble. 'See what you've done for me. And a few months ago no one thought I'd ever walk again.' But at the Gunnedah Abbattoir she changes her white coat for the grey coat and soft cloth cap all those entering the building must borrow from the sewing room. She flies there if the weather is right and her husband is not flying somewhere else in their plane. But on wet days, or on very early starts when she would have to take off from a farm strip in the dark, she drives a car.

The abattoir is especially grim in the early morning. She walked up a short flight of cement steps, pushes open a steel swing door that leads to more steps. The disinfecting gang has been at work during the night. Grey walls hang with the grey-white foam they spray. It spreads across the steps and blurs them. Grey clouds hedge the corridors, diminish the great dressing room. She walks upward into an atmosphere as sombre as a tomb.

When she slides open the door of the chiller, it might be a morgue with 700 bodies hanging from hooks that slide on overhead rails. The distributing fans of the refrigerator roar uncomfortably loudly. A light, white, frosty mist moves about the room. The temperature is 0°C. She almost closes the door behind her to maintain the temperature. What if someone came along, did not see her in the fog at the far end of the room, and locked the door? One man shut in such a chiller at twelve o'clock on the Friday afternoon of a long weekend, knew he would die if he stopped moving. He shifted carcasses from one rail to the next, and when he had moved them all one way, he moved them back. After forty hours an electrician unexpectedly opened the door to check on something. He survived.

Kerry Jane works with a knife in one hand, a torch in the other. The powerful fluorescent lights overhead do not reach far enough into the carcass cavities. She cuts out missed collapsed bladders, small bruises, grass seeds. A Californian diner would raise hell if he found a spear grass seed in his expensive rack of lamb. After several hours, Kerry cannot feel her toes, she cuts her frozen fingers. At that temperature she cannot wear the steel mesh gloves the workers in the warmer boning room wear. The gloves stick to flesh.

During the afternoon nine or ten girls come in to pull cheesecloth stockinettes, branded with RICH MEATS PTY LTD, over the passed carcasses. They chatter bawdily and loudly to make themselves heard above the refrigerator noises and reveal astonishingly intimate knowledge about most of the men in the abattoir.

'Goin' out with 'Arry tonight. What's 'e like when 'e's got a girl on her own?'

'Which 'Arry do you mean—six-inch 'Arry or eight-inch 'Arry?'

One girl had trouble pulling the bags on. 'You've got to pull them right up,' explained Kerry Jane. 'All the flesh has to be covered. You can't leave the legs poking out.' The girl had worked for months lifting brains out of split heads and throwing them into a dish. 'Don't like workin' up here,' she complained to a workmate. 'Gotta think too much. All I had to do down there was pick and flick.'

Two Japanese buyers flew out from Japan to inspect the last kill. They felt the fat, they smelt their fingers. They took video film. They stroked the flesh, they smelt their fingers. They took video film. They touched fat again, they smelt their fingers. They took video film. Apparently the smell of these carefully fed lambs did not offend them. They gave a small weekly order to find out whether Japanese housewives could bear the smell of it cooking.

*It is superior stock,
the product of our paddocks.
We grew it*

Packaged food repels me, especially the foam trays of sliced meat covered with plastic on supermarket shelves. It looks artificial. I expect to turn a tray over and see 'Manufactured by the Edulia Chemical Company' stamped on the bottom, or 'Caro Prime Cuts Inc., the makers of better-than-nature products'. Good food exhibits its origins. Potatoes with a dusting of the soil they grew in look better than their scrubbed and washed companions. The soil flavours them more than sunlight, as it flavours a peanut or a truffle. So let them show it.

I have just finished writing a long chapter on Chinese food for the human history of the Chinese in Australia that I have been working on for years. Since so few families own refrigerators in China, they buy their flesh alive. One can stand on street corners and watch the evening meals pedalling home: a live carp flapping from one handlebar balanced by a pinioned duck on the other, a box of live frogs on a rear rack, a turtle or two, a chicken in a cage or a sucking pig, and always big bunches of vegetables tied on somewhere.

A seller of quail in Macao skinned his birds for his customers. He reached into a cage of live birds, drew one out, turned it over, slipped the long thumbnail on his left hand under the skin on its neck, grasped the skin between thumb and forefinger and peeled the bird in one quick movement. He stripped the wings in two strokes and dropped it into a plastic bag. I expected to see the naked birds make grotesque attempts to fly out but the skinning killed more quickly than if he had cut their heads off.

It is a delight to watch knowledgeable Hong Kong housewives buying frogs from a street stall. The vendor has his big cages encroaching on the road. Some Hong Kong streets end up as metre-wide paths. Stall fronts stall fronts shop. A buyer goes down on her knees, studies the winding and entwining frogs. 'That one.' She points to one with fat thighs. The stallholder reaches in, seizes one. 'No! No! That one!' She has followed it over, under, through a maze of frogs. Finally she has the half dozen she wants and carries them home in a squirming plastic bag.

The pigeon sellers in Central markets feed thousands of squabs each late afternoon. Men and women sit on low stools, tiers of round cane baskets a metre in diameter and full of pigeons on one hand, empty baskets on the other. In front on a low table is a dish of soaked grain barely covered with water. A feeder catches a bird in one hand, opens its beak, bends forward, sucks up grain and water into his own mouth, squirts it down the pigeon's open beak, then tosses the bird into an empty cage. The squabs are very quiet, and, although at a few weeks they are fully feathered, they make no attempt to fly away.

In the best fish restaurants one enters through a bubbling corridor of glass tanks, displaying all that one might eat: saltwater fish, freshwater fish, huge prawns, little prawns, turtles, fat eels, thin eels, mussels, fan shells, shrimps, live crabs running over one another, and giant sulky crabs with their claws trussed to their shells.

Both buyer and seller in China know where their food comes from. Even when brought to the table a sliced turtle is put together again and its shell placed over the top. A platter of eight sliced pigeons look ready to fly away. Heads poke out one side, legs trail out the other, the wings are opening. Fish come complete with heads. Indeed, some species have the finest flesh in their cheeks.

I killed a lamb a few days ago. That used to be a weekly or twice-weekly chore. Since Joan, my vital wife, grew sick and died I lived alone and did not kill for myself. Elaine came to sort my mass of Chinese papers and arrange them in chapters. She stayed to wait the end of the book, the beginning of the next, the next. The farm came to life again. We saw a good lamb in the paddock. I killed it.

I made stock of the four shanks, the heart, flaps, diaphragm, brisket, neck, sweetbreads and head, with parsley, bay leaves, pepper and unpeeled onions sliced in quarters. Somehow the head came to the top. When I took the lid off to skim the scum the eyes watched me, teeth considered the onions splitting into concentric arcs. It is superior stock, the product of our paddocks. We grew it.

In a village on the Tan River in the Pearl River delta women gathered about us as we watched a dog butcher at work. 'Have you eaten dog?' they asked us. 'It is good, good. It is our food. By the time you've eaten half a dog you know where heaven is.'

*Flocks of these birds
dance in graceful patterns . . .*

A Pallid Cuckoo called on the morning of 1 September. Here, this bird announces spring, but it is seldom so particular about dates. It has no regular migratory pattern—it leaves some districts, stays in others. It always leaves this place about mid-April and returns in the fast-growing weather between the first week in August and the last week in September, whenever there is that spring lift in the air and soil. Its first calls are a delight, a few musical notes down the scale, then back again to the starting point and a few notes higher. But like all cuckoos it never knows when to stop. It begins at daylight and continues every minute or two all day and well into the night. People call it the Brainfever Bird.

Distinctly barred on breast and long tail, the male has a hawk-like appearance in flight. He makes use of this when his mate is ready to lay. He swoops on a nesting Mudlark or Grey Fantail. The agitated female leaves her eggs to chase him, her watching mate joins in. He leads them away and keeps them occupied while his mate slips in, quickly lays an egg and flies off with one of the others in her beak. Birds can count but they do not seem able to reason that the cuckoo's egg is bigger than the one they laid. The sturdy young cuckoo has a sensitive spot on the back of its neck. When one of the other nestlings falls across it, the uncomfortable cuckoo braces its legs, shuffles till it has the offending nestling squarely on its back, stands up, takes a step backwards, and flings it out of the nest. Soon one lone, big cuckoo fledgling fills the nest and squawks for food.

And one male White-winged Triller has turned up, calling 'joey, joey' during the day and making his long, musical two-note trill in the early morning. Some years none of these birds come here

*Some years none of these birds
come here at all*

at all, some years they come in numbers. Will a late female find this one male, or will he spend a long summer alone?

Driving in a little-used forest a couple of months ago, I came on a Mallee Fowl, the first I have ever seen, feeding in the middle of the track. It—the sexes are indistinguishable unless one can watch their behaviour on the wonderful nesting mounds they build—was unconcerned about me. I pulled up about ten metres away and watched it, moving up slowly as it walked down the road. After about twenty minutes I got out of the Landcruiser and walked towards it. It moved off among the bloodwood and blackboys, still feeding but keeping the same ten metres in front. After a while it flew, much like a domestic fowl but higher, over the trees, then up two to three hundred metres over a little hill and away.

Sixty years ago they used to fly out of the then open forest in the late afternoon and eat wheat with domestic fowls on farms. In the 1940s they seemed to disappear under the grey blanket of rabbits. Now, astoundingly, they have come back and are spreading. No one had seen a Mallee Fowl in that area for over sixty years.

A few days ago, David Hadfield, a near neighbour, rang us to say that a couple of Brolgas had visited his farm. Elaine and I drove over to see them. They were feeding along a fence line. Elegant grey birds, they stood so tall to watch us when they heard the vehicle, the pink collar on their upper necks lifted level with the top barb of the fence. Flocks of these birds dance in graceful patterns of wing-spreading, long-stepping, bowing and turning. A bird that gets out of line is pecked back into place. They used to be common in New South Wales, then disappeared for years. But the birds that come here now are nervous. We could not approach closer than a kilometre before they flew. The draining of swamps in northern Queensland has interfered with their breeding. In the non-breeding season they collect in flocks of a thousand or so in the north of Western Australia and feed on crops. Farmers poison them and shoot them. They are decreasing in Australia now. David's wary visitors have probably been displaced from the north.

In January 1971 we had an extraordinary visit of north Queensland butterflies. Heavy, warm, cyclonic rain swept down from Cooktown, through central Queensland into New South Wales and bore Australian Crows, Common Eggflies and the spectacular, fast-flying Blue Tigers with it. A big crop of grapes near the house fermented and the butterflies stayed to feast on the rotting fruit. For a fortnight the garden smelt like a winery and the air was striped with Blue Tigers.

*They like to have
their saws screaming
by first light*

*The sleeper cutter
Pulls a little rope
To start the motor
Of his chainsaw,
Braw-w-w, like an early morning alarm.*

*He guns the finger throttle
And the ricocheting echoes
Rattle round him through the forest.*

I began that unfinished poem some years ago. I ought to work on it again.

Baradine, our little local town that grew up on soft, yellow, fragrant White Cypress Pine now feeds on dense, red Narrow-leaf Ironbark, one of the hardest of all timbers. The sleeper cutters begin moving out in the dark to harvest it. They like to have their saws screaming by first light. They will have spent a couple of days blazing the straight, sound trees that will yield them their month's quota for the railways. Most of them work alone, some with an offsider. A man walks to a tree he has blazed carrying his saw at the idle, he turns it on its side, revs it up, and makes a cushioning cut across what he has judged to be the line of fall, then he pulls the saw free, swings it round to the opposite side, grips the throttle on full revs, applies the blade about ten centimetres higher than the first cut, and slices through the tree. It squeaks, it groans, its top trembles a little, it crashes with a concertinaed thud, leaves crumbling, twigs bending, branches breaking, trunk collapsing among them. The ironbark, named for its black, deep-furrowed bark, has been growing for one or two hundred years. The saw has stopped its growth in seconds. The great tree lies there, blacker than its shadow ever was, among the grey uniformity of early morning. The sleeper cutter trims off useless side branches, tops it where it narrows to less than sleeper thickness, squares off the butt, then moves on to his next blazed tree. His offsider in an old diesel tractor, mudguards dented, tyres torn, jam tin exhaust cover dangling by a bit of wire, snigs the logs to a central clearing and barks them ready for the power saw. They look strangely naked, white, smooth, damp and pimpled, as though goosefleshed by the sudden uncovering.

The sleeper cutter has raked the sawing area then swept it as fussily as last century's housewives swept their verandahs. Power saws can pick up a chip or a big stick and hurl it back like a cannon shell. He props a log clear of the ground, marks out the sleepers in it (they have to be free of sapwood), chops a sighting groove in the near end with a tomahawk, drives a chip as marker into a groove in the far end, lines up his big saw and rips off the first offcut. Ironbark sleepers are superior despite BHP's invitations to join the modern age with steel.

But the heart of Baradine, now so many pine mills have closed down, is the Gallagher Insultimber mill, making ironbark electric fence posts. This timber, wet or dry, does not conduct electricity. Roy Matthews, enthusiastic, energetic, hard hat on his head, cordless telephone in his hip-pocket, runs one of the best-equipped mills in Australia. Since the posts are small in section, he can make use of the trees unfit for sleepers—the hollow, the bent, the twisted, the cracked.

A big forklift makes the first move. It carried several logs up to a wide steel elevator. From then on everything moves in a smooth flow. The big logs travel into the debarking machine where knives strip the bark off. The bark travels back into a grader and chopper that sieves out the dust and feeds the clean pieces on to a pile for sale as garden mulch. The logs come out of the machine

. . . now so many pine mills have closed down . . .

looking as prickly as sheepsfoot rollers—the knives gouge up splinters from the sapwood. They travel down to an operator on a big electrical chainsaw who cuts them into lengths, then feeds them on to another operator on a computerised double saw. He touches buttons that give him exquisite control. Two arms pick up the log, level it, present it to the saw that can be adjusted to fractions of a millimetre. Here a rectangular length of solid timber is prepared. The offcuts drop on to a chain leading to the chip mill. A hundred cubic metres move out by tipper each morning on their way to Japan. Ironbark makes the finest paper.

A gang saw working up and down like a line of old crosscut saws divides the big blocks into post widths. They move on till they are pointed, drilled, grooved, trimmed to length, bound in bundles.

The posts go all over the world. Baradine ironbark winters under snow in Iceland while the stock are shedded, then, in the summer thaw, the fences grow out of the ground again with the bright new pasture.

One savours sweet air
and a memory of
rich wine

D r Nathan Pritikin advised that one should regard the yolk of an egg as cyanide.

When I went on to my first block of land in 1948, Bowy Nott, a neighbouring farmer, advised me, 'If you want to work hard, Eric, you've got to get a good breakfast inside you—thirteen eggs and a pound and a half of steak.' He stood almost two metres tall even though a cranky working bullock had gored him in the back of the neck when he was young and bowed his head forward. He out-worked two good men as a matter of course, three or four when he was showing off. The rest of his family did not match his egg-eating, but a normal breakfast used five or six dozen eggs. Their vegetable garden bore witness: they used the shells as mulch. Cabbages and lettuce seemed to grow on a reef of glistening white coral.

Bowy thrived to a good age. So we have not renounced our mayonnaise or garlic dressing. I sit with a bowl between my knees, wire whisk in my right hand, jug of first pressings olive oil in my left. I stir the two or three egg yolks in the bowl, add a drop of oil, stir, drop, stir, drop, stir, slurp, add a teaspoon of crushed garlic, stir, slurp, stir, add more oil, more garlic, more oil, more garlic. Three ingredients that look incorrigibly disparate mould into something yellow, smooth, thick, new and delicious. And a teaspoon of water at the end somehow makes them inseparable.

And occasionally we serve zabaglione to our guests with no fear of poisoning them. It is fun making it to end a good dinner, measuring sugar and madeira (more delicate than the recommended marsala) in half eggshells to go with the yolks and whisking them in a double boiler with a little

*. . . stood quietly with beaks pointed
at a disdainful angle*

electric mixer till the froth reaches the top and holds its peaks when I lift the whisk. Eat at once. It is so light it can barely be felt in the mouth. One savours sweet air and a memory of rich wine.

We recently added some new hens to the poultry yard. The only sensible laying fowls to buy now are those computer-designed marvels, the egg-laying strain, bred for light weight, small appetite, no brooding and many big eggs. Being sensible for too long at a time grows boring. We bought four Minorca pullets from Ted Taylor, a nearby farmer who breeds them and shows them.

Our hens had grown sedate. We find we cannot ruthlessly make soup stock of them and replace them when they reach two years of age and pass their prime. We keep them till they die. Even the egg-laying strain have grown matronly. The Rhode Island Reds and Light Sussex are middle-aged haughty. They scratch with considered caution and only when they are sure there is something worth scratching for. They ease themselves into a dust bath and fluff up two or three feathers modestly at a time. They cluck quietly, squawk seldom.

The sleek black Spanish pullets from the island of Minorca danced among them, huge combs with flamboyant points flaring red, massive white ear pieces swinging. They squawked in loud, high-pitched tones. Then they began to rake over the yard. Lean, elegant legs swung rhythmically, heads bobbed in flashes of red, black and white. The other fowls retired into a corner and stood quietly with beaks pointed at a disdainful angle. Eyes flashed consternation, then steady disapproval.

Eggs mean chickens and chickens mean many good recipes. Our fennel in the garden is ready to eat after months of waiting. Elaine cooked the young bulbular stem bases as she cooks witloof or artichokes and served them with chicken braised in cream and white wine and dusted over with tiny green feathers of chopped fennel leaves. The faint taste of aniseed produced a new chicken.

When we mate game roosters with our mixed fowls we get chickens of all colours, striped, splotched, pale blue, pale pink. They look like a yard full of butterflies. The sensible chicken to buy is the giant meat crossbred, ready in weeks instead of months. And yes, they are superb eating. But the computer that bred them forgot to specify that legs are for walking on. Heavy legs fold under some of their heavy bodies and they walk about on their shanks.

In time, so I read, efficiently produced chickens will have no wings, no legs, no feathers. They will grow on the end of a feed tube. I think my appetite will wane.

Letting the grass grow
solves the problem . . .

In the late 1850s homesick South Australian sportsmen released hares to breed at The Reedbeds. They were expected to improve the shooting. Now their unmolested descendants stand on hind legs to watch the planes land on the drained swamps that have become the suburb of West Beach, and Adelaide's airport.

But it is the Silver Gull that especially finds airports a good feeding ground. They land in thousands on the flat, mown expanses and have to be moved out of the path of the planes. At Heathrow and Gatwick in England, where northern hemisphere gulls are attracted, authorities have revived the old sport of falconry. Magnificent Peregrines are trained to make low sweeps across the fields. The gulls fly off screaming their alarm and the falcons return to their handlers to perch on steel mesh gloves and receive titbits of mice as reward.

At Wynyard in Tasmania, where my son Mitchell monitors planes in and out as a flight service officer, plovers as well as gulls have moved in. The plovers are no danger. They keep to the grass, even sit on their eggs in a hollow in the ground a few centimetres off the edge of a runway. The gulls take to the air unwarily and as many as ten have been hit by an incoming plane. The ground staff drive around firing off pistols loaded with Bird Frite that causes insufficient fright. Letting the grass grow solves the problem at some fields. Gulls do not like walking about on grass fifteen centimetres high. But most keepers of airports, as well as the birds, find unmown grass unattractive.

Pilots of planes big and small report to a local controller when they take off—they give destination, route and estimated time of arrival at key points. They report again on landing so that Search and Rescue do not go out looking for an overdue plane.

Pilots running heroin between Port Moresby and lonely northern Australian strips give their destination as the Trobriand Islands where there is no radio. Out of sight of Port Moresby, they turn south instead of north, then in forty minutes report a landing in the Trobriands. They continue on, make their drop, pick up a suitcase of notes, perhaps a crate of rare parrots, and head north. On the way home they announce a take-off from the Trobriand strip, and forty minutes later land as innocents in Port Moresby.

An inexperienced pilot that a friend of Mitchell's was controlling kept revising her estimated time of arrival at Katoomba. 'Confirm operations normal. Are you aware of your present position?' he asked her several times. 'Yes! Yes!' she answered confidently. After half an hour he knew something was wrong and called her again. 'My revised estimate is arrive Katoomba in ten minutes,' she assured him. 'Go ahead your present position.' Then she burst into tears. 'Oh Sydney, I don't know where I am. I could be anywhere.' Radar is called in before the search planes go up. Her green blob showed up on a screen not too far off course, and they directed her in safely.

On a particularly busy day in Sydney a few years ago a farmer pilot asked Mitchell for clearance. Mitchell answered in a burst of quick directions. 'Enter controlled air space. Track via Bindook, then the 062 localiser to Sydney. Enter at 7000, contact control on 123 decimal 9.' There was silence. The pilot should have acknowledged his level. Mitchell called him. 'Sydney,' he answered, ponderously deliberate, 'see—how—I—talk—that's—how—I—listen—would—you—say—again—please?'

Fog sometimes confuses experienced pilots. A twin-engine plane with a full complement of passengers came in one night to a southern strip and asked permission to land. The operator reported dangerous fog and advised the pilot to go on to another town about 200 kilometres away. The pilot, on a tight schedule, was unwilling. He could see the lights of the town clearly as he circled, he could see the strip, even the lights in the control tower. He came in to land. The operator could see him, too, while he looked up. He nervously watched him begin his descent, come lower, lower.

Then his angle of vision grew too oblique to see through the fog. The plane with its rows of lights vanished abruptly. He saw it next parked on the strip about 100 metres from his tower.

The shaken pilot and co-pilot explained that they could see perfectly until they hit 150 feet then it seemed a white sheet was pulled over their heads. They put on full power to lift up, hit the runway with a mighty bump and decided to stay down, braking as hard as it was safe.

Despite the intensive training of pilots and air traffic controllers, administrators accept that accidents can happen. A doctor told me that the morgue at Glebe was designed to hold two full 747s.

*Ever since man
has travelled by sea
he has carried animals*

Two and a half thousand years ago Phoenician mariners in ships built by master craftsmen rounded the Cape of Good Hope and brought back apes and peacocks from India to confirm the wonders overseas. The great Chinese eunuch, Zheng He, with his organs preserved in a little clay pot tied to his waist so that he would not go incomplete to the next world, led out a convoy of sixty-two ships manned by 27,000 men and sailed to East Africa in the 1420s. Among a cargo of plants, rare timbers, pepper, they brought back ostriches, zebras, antelopes, and a giraffe that paraded to marvelling crowds through the streets of Nanking. They carried enough seed to grow fresh vegetables for all the men on board, but how did they feed a giraffe its special diet of grass and topmost leaves for the nine long months of the return journey?

Indonesian fishermen who come down to collect trepang in waters illegally close to Australia's north-west coast bring cages of little red hens that they sometimes take ashore to the consternation of customs officers. The red cocks make the journey in cages at the top of the masts. They crow when land is in sight, explain the fishermen who travel without instruments, not even a compass. But they know long before their cocks crow where land is. They read the shape of waves and the direction of waves and the almost imperceptible deflected swells that move under them.

Ever since man has travelled by sea he has carried animals. The ancestor of every exotic animal in Australia came by sea. But there have been appalling losses of animals and men aboard ships. In the seventeenth century, when sailors were regarded as the scum of the earth and expendable,

Spanish captains on the two-year Manila–Acapulco run regularly lost about forty per cent of their men. Captain Traill of the *Neptune* in the Second Fleet clamped his convicts in irons made for negro slaves and left them to rot for the eight-month voyage. Nearly half of them died on the way out. Of those who arrived alive in June 1790 few could walk, most died in a year or two.

If men were expendable, animals were not. Their death was somebody's monetary loss. So Gregory Blaxland carried his swarm of bees in his cabin when he sailed to Sydney in 1806. One hundred and thirty-two Zebu cattle brought from Bengal in 1795 had twenty attendants to feed and soothe them. Windsails supplied fresh air. Each time the ship tacked, the attendants turned the cattle comfortably up the slope of the deck.

But more than half the Merino sheep that Captains Kent and Waterhouse tried to bring from South Africa in 1797 died when storms doubled the time of the passage. For the last five weeks the sheep had to live 'on air most of the time'. Nine nervous hares consigned to Tasmania in 1868 made a safe journey until New Year's Day when the din of drums, horns and shouts of celebrating sailors so panicked them they all died. No one knew that hares cannot abide noise.

When the modern live sheep exports began, no one knew that sheep suffered so much from seasickness, that stress so predisposed them to respiratory disease, and that salmonella spread so violently. Sheep were run aboard in thousands without preconditioning; urine and faeces loaded with bacteria dropped through the decks from top to bottom. On one ship 5000 died out of 100,000, most of them on the bottom deck. The stewards hauled the bodies up a painful series of steep steps and threw them overboard. In the interests of the animals, of their keepers, of profit, no one wanted a repeat of those losses. Sheep now are conditioned in huge sheds then loaded aboard into pens where humidity and temperature are designed to suit them. Except in heavy conditions when sheep give in, losses are few.

Brian Ford, a friend from Kangaroo Valley, made several trips to Japan a few years ago with horses and cattle. They are loaded into open containers that are hoisted on deck and roped down. The first trip with horses was difficult. They have to be tied in place so they do not fight and too many horses were given incompatible companions. It soured their tempers. The anger spread. At the end of the journey, said Brian, it was like feeding cages of wild tigers. If he had put an arm too near as he fed them, a horse would have ripped it off. Nervous and bad-tempered horses are now excluded. All know one another before they go aboard.

The big bullocks out of a Quirindi feedlot travelled calmly. They soon learnt that there was room in each container for five to lie down while two stood up, so they took it in turns to sleep. The prone bodies worried one of the Japanese sailors at night. Brian was shaken awake with shouts of 'Cattle all dead! Cattle all dead!' So he had to go on deck and wake a few up to prove they lived. Near Papua New Guinea the heat worried them on some trips. Brian added electrolytes to their water, hosed them down with fresh water. Sometimes one died on a trip, never more.

The campaign against the export of live animals from Australia is not sensible. We have 2500 years of experience and much modern knowledge to give them safe passage.

*Their job
is much more exacting
than that of a doctor*

Kim, my elder son, was called to a busy Sydney veterinary clinic in the early hours of the morning a few years ago after he had slept for only an hour or two. So he scarcely noticed the clients who were telling him over and over, 'Our poor little doggie is so sick, so sick,' and handing him a still form wrapped up in a blanket. Kim put it on his inspection table and unrolled a basset hound so fat it looked like a barrel with four paw-shaped stands under it. 'Oh Lord, she's fat!' said Kim. 'I don't see why she should be,' said one of her owners sharply, 'she only eats what we eat.' Kim looked up to the two fattest women he had ever seen. He wondered how they fitted through the door.

And an agitated man rang to say his Chihuahuas had somehow got stuck together and they were making excited noises. 'Where are they?' asked Kim. 'Right here,' the man said. 'I've got one in each hand and the phone under my chin.' Kim explained the strange technique of mating dogs, as he explained to the woman who came in crying with her Pomeranian. 'She's all swollen and sore.' 'Where?' 'Here,' she said and turned her bitch around. All Kim could see under her tail was cotton wool and bandaids. He unsnagged them from the hair. 'She's on heat,' he said. 'Heat? What's that?'

In England where he worked for a year or so he was called to a flamingo with a broken leg, and often out to farmhouses to treat wild hedgehogs. All England fosters hedgehogs. British Rail carries the injured free to special Hedgehog Centres for treatment. Farmers entice them to their back

They treat horses, cattle, sheep . . .

doors and feed them scraps. They are subject to ticks, lice and fleas, and sometimes their skins become so irritated they get flyblown. So Kim dusted colonies of them with powder or dipped them in special solutions.

At evening clinic, after a day in the field, he might find sixty or seventy people waiting with an assortment of animals. But luckily many of them could be dealt with quickly. They had brought in their pet tortoises for pre-winter injections of vitamins to tide them over their hibernation.

Now Kim works with Ross Pedrana in a busy, widespread practice at Narromine. They treat horses, cattle, sheep, goats, pigs, poultry, caged birds of many species, cats, dogs—every animal man associates with. Veterinary surgeons have to know so much anatomy. Their job is more exacting than that of a doctor. A safe cut on one species of animal would sever an artery on another. Each animal needs different handling, and sick animals are often more nervous than healthy animals. Breeds of dogs have different temperaments. A Brahmin bull can strike with its front legs like a camel, its hind legs kick out at different angles from a Hereford's. Some city-born veterinary surgeons never learn to handle horses. A flighty thoroughbred that stands calmly for someone who approaches it quietly and confidently might rear and strike at one who is nervous.

The attention that animals get by the best veterinarians is on the same scale of knowledge and skill as that given by the best doctors. Every technique of human medicine is paralleled in animal medicine. Hip replacements are successful in Labradors, a breed with a congenital deformity. The surgeon always advises that the dog be sterilised at the same time so it cannot pass on its defect.

Dairy farmers on the coast are now selling out and moving on to the good, comparatively cheap land at Narromine. Trying to run a rural enterprise on land valued at $10,000 a hectare is hopeless. So now Kim makes very early monthly starts at dairies and examines each cow as she comes from the bail, to record her calving date, serving date, health, production, to test her for pregnancy. All information is fed to a computer run by the Dairy Herd Health Scheme in Queensland.

The chief disadvantage of a country veterinary practice, and there seems no way out of it, is the driving, driving, driving. Despite routines, a radio network, and many telephone calls, it can happen that a farmer finds a sick beast in an area 100 kilometres away that Kim has just returned from. On his worst day he drove 500 kilometres as well as working for ten hours.

He rang a few nights ago to say another grandchild is due next April. I already have three exceptional grand-daughters. It is more than likely that there will be a fourth. The less robust male genes cannot cope with the fumes of halothane, the volatile anaesthetic generally used for both animals and humans.

*. . . we head roughly north
to find unknown wonders*

Twenty years ago, Joan, Kim and I packed a new Land Rover with drums of petrol and water, with spare parts, cameras, sleeping-bags and notebooks, with stores for six weeks in case rain cut us off somewhere, with a hired transceiver that worked to the Flying Doctor base, with fishing rods and mussels and worms to catch yellowbelly in the Cooper, and headed north-west. I had written 80,000 words of *They All Ran Wild* and needed to interview doggers, brumby shooters and rabbiters for some of the rest. Beyond the area we were to work in we had planned nothing. What turned up was more than I ever hoped for.

Now Elaine and I have fitted up a Toyota Landcruiser with winch, refrigerator, extra battery, extra fuel tank, tent, generator, stove, spare parts, books, cameras, powerful CB radio, fishing rods and reels, and headed north-east as far as Brisbane. I have written 80,000 words of a human history of the Chinese in Australia and need to see where they mined in Queensland and the Northern Territory before I write the mining chapters. This is the first of a series of travelling diaries.

We are heading to the Palmer River to see what is there before the rains cut us off, then west across the gold country to Darwin. Then we work south out of the wet season. Beyond that we have arranged nothing. Timetables and planned routes based on what we know now might exclude what we do not know.

Somewhere on the Palmer River, where the map shows contours so close they run into each other, the Chinese built remarkable aqueducts with stone-pitched walls on the lower side up to ten metres high. A procession of hundreds bore stones to the masons.

In many parts of Australia the Chinese ran channels up to forty kilometres long. They pegged them out with a level consisting of a rice bowl fixed in the centre of a 1.8 metre plank and filled with water to a marked line. The correct fall was shown by lifting the plank till the water reached the rim on the lower side. There are stories that they were so good they could run water uphill.

The best aqueducts I have seen yet are out of Tenterfield in the New England district. Creeks still follow the new paths the Chinese cut for them with picks and shovels over a hundred years ago. In the Boonoo Boonoo area to the north a natural granite wall held back a rich slide of gold and soil from a low hill. A small creek fed by a spring-filled swamp ran through the valley at the bottom of the hill. The gold-diggers began at the swamp and cut a channel a metre wide and up to six metres deep across a series of low ridges to where they needed washing water. Then they dammed off the head of the natural creek and opened their channel into the swamp. To release the tail water they cut through the granite wall.

At Surface Hill to the south-east of Tenterfield they dammed One Mile Creek and turned it through the intervening ridge across country they wanted to sluice into Nelson Creek that ran at a lower level. It would be dangerous to walk that country at night. Wherever there are rocks the creek flows through a gash as it was originally cut, ten metres deep and two-thirds of a metre wide. The softer banks have fallen in but the fast-flowing water has swept the soil away and kept the channel open. The bottom is a different world. Direct sunlight never reaches it. It is always cool and moist in a land hot and dry in summer, cold and dry in winter. One looks down on a miniature rainforest. Tree ferns grow there and giant mosses among many smaller plants.

Before we leave Brisbane, Elaine and I have to unpack, weigh everything, then repack somewhat less. With empty water containers, without the essential, second spare wheel and several other things, we are startled to find we have reached maximum weight. I had not finished a chapter I was working on so I packed some books. I have to give a talk in Darwin, so I packed some more. Lest I miss information for this diary, I packed some more. I packed too many.

So when we have repacked the right essentials, we head roughly north to find unknown wonders.

*The Aborigines, too,
treated the trees
with special care*

On the edge of a steep piece of council land in the heart of suburban Brisbane there are two healthy Bunya Pines, the striking trees that were so important to Aboriginal culture. In a society where land and food was usually common property, each man owned two or three of these trees and handed them down to his son. Every third year, when they bore a prolific crop of nuts, other tribes were invited to a feast. Hundreds, sometimes thousands, came in from up to 200 kilometres away.

The trees grew in scattered places along a short section of the slopes and ranges of south-east Queensland. They probably never numbered more than several hundred. The local tribes knew every tree. Because they were so valuable to the Aborigines, the Queensland government protected them.

The Aborigines, too, treated the trees with special care. When climbing they usually cut toe notches with an axe while supporting themselves with a vine rope looped around waist and trunk. But they feared to wound the Bunyas and climbed with rope only. Although the sandpapery bark gave a good grip, the trees were an uncomfortable climb for a naked man, since the narrow, glossy, deep-green leaves have sharp spikes on the end.

The nuts ripened about January. As the owner-climber threw down the laden cones from thirty to forty metres up, those below split them open, ate a few raw, but put most of them in dillybags to be roasted later at the camp. The feast went on for days, supplemented with fruit and game. Then, in another most unusual practice, they reserved big quantities of the nuts, and stored them under water to be eaten about two months later when they had germinated and were soft and cheesy.

The beautiful Norfolk Island Pine is a member of the same genus, as is the Hoop Pine that produces such magnificent timber. 'A noble specimen,' reported the judge at the London International Exhibition in 1862, 'remarkable for the peculiar figure set up by a series of remote, small, pea-shaped, pale, clouded knots, arranged in quincunx order, somewhat like drops of rain in general effect.'

Elaine and I drove out to Brookfield, an outer Brisbane suburb, to see a reserve of Hoop Pines that her grandfather, W. R. Moon, once owned. In 1959 he founded the National Trust of Queensland and handed over the three-hectare plantation to them. A little creek runs through it where English watercress thrives. The creek once ran wider and deeper and the cress grew so prolifically W. R. fed it to his milking cows in dry times. Elaine's mother and aunt pitchforked loads of it into a horse-drawn dray.

The Trust has done nothing with the reserve. People run horses and cattle on it and they destroy the litter. The land grows mostly weeds. Apart from the pines, it is difficult to find a native plant. But Brush Turkeys breed there. We watched a male working on his mound.

He was in fine plumage, polished black with deep red head and neck. The thick, rounded apron that hangs across his breast flared bright yellow with a V-shaped streak of red at the centre as though his neck was bleeding down it. He raked leaves vigorously and noisily. It sounded like a big animal thrashing about. The mound was about four metres in diameter but only two thirds of a metre high. Perhaps it is a first season mound. After several years they reach four or five metres.

The female approached. He threw out his wings and chased her away. If the fermenting leaves have not yet raised the temperature high enough, she cannot be allowed to think about laying. His violence discourages her until the time is right.

These birds are naturally shy and difficult to observe. One crawls through rainforest, one waits in silence for a glimpse. In Brisbane they have maintained their presence wherever there is a patch of bush and they are almost domesticated. The traffic halted in busy Caxton Street a couple of days ago to allow a wandering male to cross.

*You're booming in here
right now. You're pushing
just on seven*

'How yer goin', Smoky? This is Dave 'ere.'

'Go down one will yer' mate? The bloody side banders are cutting us out.'

I switched down from AM band 20 to 19 on my transmitter-receiver and continued listening. Sidebanders work on the carriers generated by extreme modulations of the high frequency standard waves.

'Do you copy me now, Smoky?'

'Yeah. I copy yer real good, mate, loud and clear. Yeah. Over.'

Once communication is established there often seems little to say. CB radio operators are long-winded, repetitive, ungrammatical, trivial, enthusiastic, patient and untiring. They chatter inconsequentially all day, all night, though they treat their equipment with great seriousness.

'It's obvious you've got a problem there. Stick to the vertical. If your needle is swinging to the red you've got more of an open circuit than a 50 ohm resistance. Yeah! You've got a problem. Stay on the vertical and let the co-ax dry out after the storm.'

On another channel Townsville worked to Dalby.

'The last couple of days haven't been too good, especially in the middle of the day. All I could get was bloody Indonesia. The buggers have no control over their power. Before that the skip was working pretty good. I was talking to Western Australia and Victoria real good and they couldn't hear one another.'

'Well, you're booming in here right now. You're pushing just on seven. The skip must be right on its peak. What sort of an aerial have you got?'

'Me! I've only got a bit of a rod.'

'Well, they talk about smoke coming off the tip of the antenna. Yours must be on fire. Now you're bending me bloody needle. You're pushing it right over.'

Radio waves can reflect off high cloud, off dense layers of air or rock faces, so that a signal that would normally vanish after 500 kilometres might skip off a reflective surface and be picked up 1000 kilometres away. The power of the transmitter and the design of the aerial control the distance that can be worked.

'I'm putting out from a thirty-five foot tower [no CB operator seems to work in metrics] with a three element beam and a stationmaster on top of that.'

'Well I'm saving a few bikkies to buy a three or four element with a rotator and all that but the bottom's fallen out of the building market up here. The boss had to lay me off and things are so crook with him he's had to put all his gear up for sale. I'm just getting by now with fortnightly cheques.'

One picks up strangely honest conversations on radio, probably because the participants talk anonymously to disembodied voices. They watch a needle that responds as they expect, not a pair of assessing eyes. I have been testing our radio and listening to procedures in case we need it. Elaine and I bought it for emergency. It would be comforting if we are sitting beside a river flooding ten kilometres wide with the road cut behind us to know if we are likely to cross it before next June. I did not know the radio world existed as it does. I had missed a startling segment of life.

A Townsville man runs regular for sale advertisements. Old men discuss their heart attacks, the young their love affairs.

"I had a few pains yesterday. Worried me a bit. I did spend a couple of days in bed last week but I think that was something else, not me heart . . .'

'He went all the way down to Kentucky Fried Chicken to see her but she wasn't there . . .'

'Oo's lookin' for Steve?'

A girl's voice cut in, 'No one's lookin' for Steve . . .'

Another girl's voice on another channel announced, 'He's no good for her.'

'That's what we all reckoned. She put on a real show, right out of control she was. So some of the boys got together, we grabbed a good hunk of timber and we walked up to his house to straighten him out but the bastard wasn't home.'

Truck drivers work Channel 8 for information, for contact in a lonely job.

'I'm running up the south-east freeway. Can someone tell me what exit ramp I take for Fisherman's Island . . . ?'

'Hey mate! Hey mate! I just seen a woman here walking down the road. She's got a see-through dress on. You can see all she's got .'

On another day a distracted truckie came back after a long pause. 'Sorry I'm late getting back to you, mate. I bloody near cleaned up a car.'

Late one night on Channel 38 an excited voice reported, 'Hey! There's a station here reckons the school's on fire.'

'Well, let 'er burn, eh?'

*. . . I had never before heard
the strange vowels of Queenslanders*

*We breakfasted on pawpaw
and pineapple ripened deliciously
on the plants*

The girl in the office said with absolute clarity, 'The editor's name is Cole MacLalland but the man you'll need to see about the old newspapers lives in 7 Alice Street.' As we walked out the door of the *Maryborough Chronicle*, Elaine, who was formerly a Queenslander, said, 'Well, the editor is Col MacLelland but we have to go up to Ellis Street.'

I knew the '-ink' for '-ing' endings of those descended from South Australia's German families but I had never before heard the strange vowels of Queenslanders. They open their mouths more when pronouncing 'o' and 'e' and short 'o' comes out long 'o', short 'e' comes out short 'a'.

Maryborough is a lovely town. Road and rail have mostly replaced the great Mary River as communication link, but timber barges from Fraser Island still dock at that part of the old long wharves that is maintained, and a big fishing fleet unloads wet fish, a term that is another Queensland peculiarity. The catch comes in fresh, not frozen. Wet Sweetlip and Coral Trout off the reef are magnificent, so are wet Mary River prawns.

Tram tracks that New South Welshmen call train lines border several streets, and little diesel engines fuss along them hauling trucks of timber, bricks, LP gas from business to business and to the main rail. The tracks once ran in from all the neighbouring sugar farms, but cane is now carried by semitrailer to Maryborough's mill.

The narrow 105 centimetre gauge makes the short trains look like toys so it is startling to see the seemingly never-ending coal trains carrying huge loads along the same width track. One train consisted of 102 trucks. A big diesel-electric engine led it in front of fifty-one trucks, three more engines were coupled in the middle followed by the other fifty-one. Three-quarters of a kilometre long, the train hauled about 2000 tonnes altogether. Walkers Ltd of Maryborough make the engines, known officially as electrical multiple units. The locals call them Emus.

Maryborough was the centre of a dugong fishery from the 1840s to the 1960s when these extraordinary creatures had grown so scarce they needed protection. My interest lies in a Chinese, Lionel Ching, who operated for over thirty years from the mid-1870s and marketed dugong oil all over the world. Rich in iodine, it has an apparently well-founded reputation as a healing ointment. The hide, two centimetres thick, makes strong, supple belting, the tusks of the male work up like attractive pink ivory, the flesh is good eating. Lionel Ching cured it like bacon.

At first he set massive nets across the mouths of tidal creeks, where the cows took their calves at high water to feed them undisturbed. With a mesh of ninety centimetres the nets were designed to let the calves and small cows through and trap the biggest. But a catch of two or three weighing over 400 kilograms each was a too heavy load to pull in and Lionel Ching, who employed Aborigines, resorted to their method of harpooning them as they fed on beds of seagrass at high tide.

Since protection, dugongs have bred up satisfactorily, especially at Burrum Heads about forty kilometres north. Hundreds sometimes flock together. But the species is not safe. Too many drown in shark nets and fish nets, too many are poached. Dredging, chemicals and muddy floodwater off agricultural land kill the seagrass, their staple food.

Elaine and I camped beside a big tidal creek in the Tuan State Forest just south of Maryborough, a place known as the Jew Hole. Wild thunderstorms proved our new tent was waterproof enough but they put the fish off the bite. We breakfasted on pawpaw and pineapple ripened deliciously on the plants. We drive north into mango country where pink Strawberry Mangoes wait for us, and red Bullock's Hearts.

*But mostly the city
is pleasantly new
and pleasantly old . . .*

Townsville is an impressive city. Over the last several years the outlandish politics of Queensland has denigrated the whole state. I expected to find that the middle and northern coast had become as garish as the Gold Coast, but Queensland's northern coastal towns are individual and beautiful, splashed with pink and red flowers, purple and yellow.

The Bohle River defines Townsville's western border though suburbs are now crossing over it, the Ross River and several creeks split it into irregular segments, Castle Hill dominates it. That rocky sculpture rises 286 metres and occupies a square kilometre in the centre of the city. It looks as though it was erected there to relieve the flatness of the town.

'I tell you what we'd do with that hill if we had it back in the States,' said a tourist. 'We'd send in the rippers and the shovels and we'd build a causeway out to your Magnetic Island. That bit of land is lost out there.'

We travelled by ferry to find it. Granite slabs and boulders spiked with Hoop Pine rise steeply out of the sea. Little beaches cut into them here and there. The water is very quiet and free of the dangerous stingers that close most northern beaches in the summer. The island copes quietly and profitably with thousands of sightseers. But a company now wants to bustle it up. NO MAGNETIC KEYS DEVELOPMENT says a big notice on the adequate narrow road that would have to be widened for a big hotel, I LIKE NELLY BAY WHERE IT IS.

The hideous Sheraton hotel and casino built on a man-made breakwater dominate the Ross River entrance. The casino is losing money fast enough to make nonsense of Sydney's grandiose and destructive plan for the world's biggest casino.

But mostly the city is pleasantly new and pleasantly old, of masonry and of timber. Houses stand airily on high stumps, roofs rise up to big, decorated iron ventilators, each one different, a special feature of Townsville. Elaine, who knows a great deal about buildings, pointed out the Victoria Park Hotel, a well-kept example of north Queensland vernacular architecture. The bottom storey is single skin timber with the studs exposed. Houses were sometimes built like that in the country. Farmer builders lined their new houses with the intention of adding weatherboards when they had the money.

Beside a modern bridge over the Ross River stands the iron Victoria Bridge completed in 1889. It is to be restored as a pedestrian crossing. The central pier houses an engine that swung the middle section of the bridge around to let boats through. Elaine rang Graham Knott, experienced in industrial archaeology, who is going to restore the engine. His enthusiasm was a delight. One of thousands produced by Crossley in Manchester, this engine might have been the only one that came to Australia. Driven by town gas, a cylinder 23 centimetres in diameter with a 60 centimetre stroke turned a flywheel 165 centimetres in diameter. This great wheel kept up a steady power to a pneumatic pump that extended the cylinder that turned the bridge. Not too many boats ever passed through. The engine driver needed an hour's notice to start the engine and build up air pressure, then, too often, Townsville's heat and the consequent expansion of the bridge sections had jammed them immovably.

The fishing fleet has its own wharves. Ships come in after two or three days or two or three weeks with prawns snap frozen in modern freezers or chilled in ice and salt as they were 100 years ago. Sometimes the captains spend a few hours handlining for reef fish and they bring in a supplementary catch. Black Kites, scavengers of all flesh, circle overhead and monitor the unloading of each ship. So does the jealous Fish Board. Sales to the public are not permitted.

The lovely Queens Park has an area of rainforest that is breaking out of its fence onto the footpath. Anderson Park displays tropic flowers. We saw a giant pandan from Cape York that had produced

Brolgas by the thousand feed and breed and dance
on the salt marshes

an extraordinary flower, the first ever under cultivation. The bright, orange, pointed petals were thirty centimetres long. No more than 100 or so of these vines are known to exist.

The great Town Common where people ran their horses and milking cows until the 1960s is now an environmental park. Brolgas by the thousand feed and breed and dance on the salt marshes. Magpie Geese come down in the wet. We found the fresh tracks of a big crocodile three kilometres from the river.

About ten per cent of Townsville's population of over 100,000 is black, most of them Torres Strait Islanders, a good-looking people. They deepen the colour of a bright city.

*In many places
the canopy closed overhead
and we drove through
green tunnels*

We had dinner in Brisbane with Marce Coomer, an old friend of Elaine's. Marce is great-niece of Teresa Rooney, who married Christie Palmerston in 1886. 'Grand-aunt Teresa was a formidable woman,' explained Marce, 'Christie had more fun with black girls. The family, timber millers in a big way, didn't approve of him at all.'

So when we got to Innisfail, instead of travelling up the coast road to Cairns, we turned west and took the Palmerston Highway up the mountains, the route he marked out in 1882 for a proposed railway. Sugar cane grows now in bright brick-red soil on smooth-topped hills and semicircular ridges. Bananas and pawpaws thrive on higher ground, then the hills run up into rough grazing with patches of dry forest. There is a little rainforest left in deep gullies and along creeks.

But the Palmerston National Park shows what was once there. Part of the new road was closed for repairs and we wound through the park on a crumbling, narrow strip of bitumen. In many places the canopy closed overhead and we drove through green tunnels.

Little ferns cover the ground. Epiphytic ferns hang on tree trunks, sprout on branches. Their fronds trail down so low they almost meet giant ferns growing up. Vines climb over everything with big, glossy palmate leaves, with scalloped leaves, round leaves, narrow leaves, fern leaves, in astonishing variety. And every tree seems different. There are eighty or more species to the hectare.

'The whole journey was one through huge jungle trees,' wrote Christie Palmerston, 'standing and upturned and wicker-worked with lawyer and bamboo canes to a denseness which can never be imagined by those who have not traversed it. The scrub-vine has a steel-like lustre of surface, that shoots the scrub-knife off in a very dangerous manner.'

Christie Palmerston was an educated man. He could describe what he saw. Prospector and adventurer, he usually travelled barefooted. Boots rotted quickly in rainforest, dry mountain slate cut them to pieces. His birth does not seem to have fitted him for rough exploring. He was the son of an exiled Italian marquis who migrated to Australia with a troupe of musicians, and Madame Carandini, the stage name of Mary Burgess who was well known as an opera singer throughout the world. Christie, too, had a good voice. It was an interest in music that attracted him briefly to Teresa Rooney.

He spoke several Aboriginal languages and got along well with them, though his authority was backed up by his rifle: 'After the skirmish, my trackers wanted to indulge in cannibalism, but I threatened to shoot the first who attempted it.'

He treated Chinese gold-diggers with the same predatory indifference. After finding doubtful traces of gold on creeks running into the short, swift Russell River south of Cairns, he put in a claim for a reward as finder of a payable goldfield and started a rush. European diggers soon returned. The country was too wild, the gold too little. So Christie with exaggerated promises persuaded Chinese storekeepers at Innisfail to fit out parties that he guided in at one pound sterling a head. For additional income he bought bullocks from an Innisfail butcher and set up his own shop on the Russell. The Chinese thought the meat too dear and tried to carry in their own. Christie sent out Aborigines to seize their meat and throw their mining tools in the river. Thereafter he issued passes, envelopes carrying tufts of cow hair, to those who dealt with him. Aborigines stationed along the tracks acted as gatekeepers.

The Johnstone River gorge that Palmerston also explored was added to the national park last August. It is the wettest part of Australia, averaging 3500 millimetres a year. In 1979, 11,000 millimetres fell there, enough water if it was confined, to reach the top of a building four storeys high. The forest is magnificent. It has never been burnt. There has been no logging. No domestic stock have run there, no feral animals have got in, no foreign plants. It is one of those rare areas of Australia that is as it was 200 years ago.

Christie Palmerston did not like it. 'Dozed off towards morning,' he wrote, 'but awoke in a short time almost suffocating, my nostrils being stuffed with clammy crawling leeches. The boys had battered decomposed logs to pieces in search of grubs. These battered substances shed broad patches of phosphoric light which gave the damp scrub a weird aspect . . . Too much parasitic verdure for my taste.'

 *We pushed our four-wheel
drives to the limit,
then we got out
and pushed ourselves*

If one stands on a knob in the Palmer River country of Cape York Peninsula one seems to be circled by concentric rings of steep ranges. Travel thirty kilometres and stand on another knob and the country has not changed.

Ridges lead nowhere. So many hills, so many gullies, so many creeks make the country as featureless as a desert. The rough grass is cinnamon-brown in the dry, green in the wet. Stunted gum grows on the creeks; spindly box, ironbark and bloodwood on the dry ridges. As over most of Australia, the thick timber is a modern growth. The miners of last century were constantly short of props and boiler fuel.

For several years in the 1870s 20,000 men worked every square metre of 10,000 square kilometres in search of gold. Every featureless feature was given two names, one by the Europeans, one by the Chinese who dominated the field seven to one. Most of the Europeans, appalled at the difficulties of the country, had rushed down to the Hodgkinson hoping to find it an easier field.

They had come up from the south unaware that the Palmer field was nearly 200 kilometres inland, unaware that they would need packhorses which were unprocurable, unaware even that there was a wet season and a dry season and that they would need six months' supplies to see out the wet. In April 1874 a mob of starving diggers rushed the SS *Florence Irving* when she docked in Cooktown and demanded to be taken south. The Queensland government paid their fares.

The Chinese had a choice of succeeding or dying. There was no government to nurture them. Some walked across from Darwin, some from New South Wales and Victoria, most came out from China. They had mortgaged their very families for fares and equipment or else they had bound themselves to wealthy shopkeepers in Australia. They were rowed towards the shore from ships anchored in deep water and thrown overboard with their equipment where the water was shallow enough to stand. They waded on to the beach, loaded from 70 to 115 kilograms on long-handled shovels as carrying-poles and set out in single file for the Palmer. They put every cubic metre of gold-bearing dirt through sluice boxes three or four times. They got about thirty tonnes of gold.

Elaine and I went in to see what traces the miners had left. John Hay, an experienced bushman, took us in. We pushed our four-wheel drives to the limit, then we got out and pushed ourselves. We had threatened our new Scarpa walking boots that if they failed to scale the Palmer we would burn them. They took us everywhere we needed to go but we felt rather foolish following behind John. He runs up two-in-one slate slopes in bare feet.

Twenty years ago he began to follow the old pack trails with a group of expert motorcycle riders. Roads wide enough to take drays were few. Even ore was carried to the batteries by packhorse, perhaps a string of 100 horses carrying 100 kilograms each. Once, following a trail in the wild Conglomerate Range, John suddenly found himself on a ridge that narrowed to less than a metre with a drop of a couple of hundred metres on each side. There was no room to stop. He was relieved when the track widened again after thirty metres.

Sam Elliott, the last of the hard rock miners in the area and a very good friend of John's, told him that modern mining companies and predatory sightseers were destroying old mining batteries, even knocking down stone walls. John formed the Palmer River Historic Preservation Society in 1982 to maintain evidence of the extraordinarily busy few years on the Palmer. The energetic society has done some remarkable work uncovering stamping mills and steam engines from a wild growth

Elaine and I went in to see
what traces the miners had left
(Photograph by Gordon Grimwade)

of exotic rubber vine, covering and restoring charcoal kilns, shovelling off thirty centimetres of soil that had covered the beautiful blue flagging in the gutters of the main street of deserted Maytown.

What did we see? We saw a little stone fortress where three Chinese crouched from Aboriginal attack, we saw many kilometres of stone walls built along creeks to stop mullock washing back over pay dirt, we saw gully dams and aqueducts cleverly placed to harvest every drop of run-off from chance dry-season storms, we saw a pile of opium tins that had been carefully flattened and stacked against a stone wall (but a mining vehicle had needlessly run over them all), we saw rows of magnificent old mango trees where Chinese gardens had been, we saw where the gods in the Maytown Temple had looked out the door onto a glorious sweep of the South Palmer and its junction with Butchers Creek.

The country now presents an anonymous face. It seems trying to deny excitement. But modern mining companies are testing to see if rich old reefs petered out where last century's miners thought they did, and still they are searching for the source of the gold that once lined the beds of creeks and rivers.

*. . . we eased ourselves
out of Atherton's superb
climate over a gravel road . . .*

We came off the Palmer River after four remarkable days with the calendar uncomfortably close to a talk, still unprepared, that I was to give in Darwin. Nevertheless we drove up to Cooktown, since we were halfway there, because we had to see the port that handled so many thousand gold-diggers. We also wanted to see their museum, which we found held a fine collection under outlandish management. Then we drove to Atherton to Peter and Jen Mansfield's beautiful avocado orchard. For five days I read and wrote and ate the best avocados I have ever tasted. Elaine interviewed Chinese, worked in libraries, got a few jobs done to the Landcruiser, and ate the best avocados she had ever tasted. The Reed variety is big and unfashionably round, hard to pack and a poor keeper, but straight off the tree it is a wonder. Peter planted a few trees for the local market.

We allowed ourselves four days to get to Darwin. Instead of following the busy bitumen road we eased ourselves out of Atherton's superb climate over a gravel road that leads through dry hills in a rain shadow. Our new map showed the road clearly. Unfortunately the map confirmed the general atrociousness of Australian road maps. The turn-off we meant to take to the main road did not exist. We pulled up outside the hotel in Irvinebank. A local had just parked. 'Can you tell me what road to take to Mount Garnet?'

'Gawd! What did you come this way for? Ah well! You've got a four-wheel drive, I suppose you'll get through. But it's forty kilometres, there are several turn-offs that go a long way nowhere, and there are no signposts. I'll tell you how to get there but you better listen.'

So we listened and we got there. But crawling up and down washed-out tracks in low range cost us 200 or 300 kilometres of the planned first day's drive. For the next two days we settled down to long hours of one hour at the wheel and one hour off and we covered nearly 2000 kilometres. The fascination of the country kept both of us alert.

Scrubs and forests in New South Wales often blur into a homogeneous grey. I do not find them monotonous because I know them so well I can make them flare with flowers out of season or hold out individual leaves to me from the mass. There is no need to imagine variety in the scrubs along the Georgetown–Normanton road. An area twenty metres square supports twenty shrubs and trees with twenty different tones of green and twenty leaf shapes. The leaves hang carelessly. There is no need for the caution of wax coats and edges turned to the sun. In the wet there is more moisture than any of them need. If the dry gets too severe they drop off.

Plumed pigeons basked on the road like lizards. They were so reluctant to leave we had to drive around them. Sometimes an Agile Wallaby, the commonest kangaroo of the north, flashed in front of us. A pretty cinnamon colour, they bend low to the ground and hop very fast, sometimes changing direction at right angles.

At Croydon we stayed in a pleasant galvanised-iron hotel with a beautiful wide-board floor, and after dinner we drove to the local cemetery and counted the Chinese graves by torchlight. The characters on the stone that might explain why the extraordinary number of 130 are buried there are too weathered to read. I will have to find out from other records. The Chinese were tribute mining on a reef field in the late 1880s and were never there in big numbers.

The road to Normanton runs beside a railway line, one of those isolated here-to-there railways peculiar to Queensland. It was intended to hook up a series of goldfields expected to yield for fifty years. They gave out as the line reached Croydon. We drove in to see the remarkable station in Normanton. Elaine as a councillor of the Queensland National Trust had a part in preserving it.

The Department of Railways, perhaps embarrassed by so obvious an embodiment of a dream, wanted to demolish it. It was intended as the big port junction. The platform is under a huge open shed with a curved roof covered by corrugated iron cut decoratively on the ends. Rust has now speckled it attractively. The offices are verandahed and roofed like a big station homestead. Engine room and workshop would have serviced many engines.

There are still spare stacks of the unique iron sleepers used on much of the track. U-shaped, they were filled with mud then inverted into place. Too tough to be eaten by termites, too heavy to wash away, they are still sound after 100 years.

We did not get to Karumba, the prawn town, where we wanted to spend a week. We did not get to Escott to fish in the Nicholson and hunt down wild bulls with wild catchers. We could not take the Burketown-Borroloola track because some of it was already under water. We have missed more than enough to bring us back.

. . . their humps flaring up impossibly,
they looked like yachts

It will be a month or two before the wind swings around and the wet monsoon bears down. But the dry is now breaking up with spectacular afternoon storms. When we crossed the Flinders River driving south to Cloncurry we were startled to find it half a banker. Then we found logs and debris strewn across floodways. The headwaters had had 150 millimetres in a late afternoon storm and during the night stretches of the road had been a metre under water. With nothing yet to hold it back, it gets away quickly.

We pulled up to allow a Bustard, the first I have ever seen, to stalk sedately across the road, and several times we had to slow down while Brolgas skipped across with outstretched wings. Black Kites or Whistling Eagles fed on every carcass. Cattle camp on the roads at night and a lot are hit by trucks.

We passed through long stretches of treeless blacksoil plains that sometimes changed to grey for a few kilometres. They carry good native grasses that are much the same as they were 200 years ago. Quiet Brahmins and Droughtmasters, the best cattle we had seen since leaving home, fed on them. Too many cattle in the north are the galloping Brahmin type, light, poor, wild and silly, dangerous stock to handle. The little bulls will stand on the side of the road and threaten vehicles as they pass.

The plains erupt suddenly into the Bang Bang Jump Up, a series of hilly mounds of loose rocks with shrubs and stunted gums growing among them. As we came down to the flats again there was a domain of ant hills, the best display of termite mounds in the whole wide region of termite mounds north of Townsville. As far as one can see there are mounds sixty centimetres to a metre high, two to three metres apart. These termites are grass eaters. Each mound holds from 100,000 to 500,000 workers. They eat more grass than any other animal.

The hills out of Mount Isa are prickly with spinifex. From a distance they look blurry. Bare rocks glint through in places. The country flattens briefly, then bulges up again repeatedly to Camooweal. There we saw our first road train: prime mover, semitrailer, then two trailers cleverly hitched so that the last trailer followed the same track as the prime mover. There were three of them in the charge of Aboriginal drivers. They were carrying 450 steers off the Barkly Tableland to fatten in Queensland.

We had dinner with a road train driver in the village pub at Larrimah. He has a contract to cart iron for bridge building from Darwin to Tennant Creek. He carries loads up to 120 tonnes. His rig is worth $500,000 and he is paying it off. He had had a long hot day and he was trying to eat enough to sustain him through another 500 kilometres by night. The kindly wife of the publican fussed over him, urging another mouthful. In five years, he said, he would be comfortable. He could give the game away.

The big run Rocklands straddles the Queensland–Northern Territory border, and the first sight of the Northern Territory suggests it is a magnificent place. Fat, quiet Santa Gertrudis cows feed over a vast blacksoil plain. Huge grey Brahmin bulls, one tonners, move among them. Long-legged anyway, but exaggerated by mirages, their humps flaring up impossibly, they looked like yachts. Rocklands also holds channel country which provides the richest feed in the world after floods to put the final polish on their cattle before market.

For the full width of the plain hundreds of Australian Dotterels rested on the road and road edges. They are very alert and took to the air in plenty of time with sharp bands of colour flashing through sharp wings, then they dived on to the road again behind us.

The country quickly changes for the worse and so do the cattle. For too long stations have run

. . . their humps flaring up impossibly,
they looked like yachts

unattended mongrels that are mustered only when prices are good. The Brucellosis and Tuberculosis Eradication Campaign, B-TEC, is changing the old methods of management. Cattle have to be mustered several times a year.

As one approaches Darwin the termite mounds grow higher and the leaves on the trees grow bigger. The mounds are built as a series of columns conjoined on the inside so that the structure becomes a deeply indented pillar up to three and a half metres tall and one and a half metres in diameter. Recent additions bulge out obviously. The deep brown soil has not had time to fade and from a distance the mounds seem to be producing grotesque bracket fungi.

Young eucalypts have leaves up to seventeen centimetres wide and twenty-seven long. All growth becomes unmistakably tropical. One is aware one is driving towards Asia.

*. . . we will enjoy Christmas
together without
a Leichhardt-like
commitment to enjoy it*

I referred to Leichhardt's *Journal of an Overland Expedition in Australia* to see what the Kakadu country looked like to the first European eyes. His writing is so interesting and so full of acute observation that I could not resist reading the whole book. Leichhardt and his party spent Christmas of 1844 east of present Emerald in Queensland. He was determined to enjoy it. In camp on 12 December he wrote, 'Our meat was all consumed; but we wished to reserve our bullocks for Christmas, which was, in every one of us, so intimately associated with recollections of happy days and merriment, that I was determined to make the coming season as merry as our circumstances permitted. This decision being final, every one cheerfully submitted to a small allowance, and did his best to procure game.'

But six days later on a series of good lagoons they forestalled Christmas and slaughtered a beast. There was water and feed enough to spend several days drying the meat. 'We feasted luxuriously on fried liver at breakfast, on stuffed heart for luncheon and on a fine steak and the kidneys for supper. Those who may have lived for so long a time as we had upon a reduced fare, will readily understand with what epicurean delight these meals were discussed.'

Christmas was an anticlimax. Leichhardt had spent several days scouting ahead and did not get back till after midday on the twenty-fifth. 'We entered our camp just as our companions were sitting down to their Christmas dinner of suet pudding and stewed cockatoo.' He did not mention New Year.

Where will Elaine and I spend Christmas? We intended to be home. To both of us family Christmases are important. But there is so much to do that it would be foolish to leave undone, it is so very far to come back, that we will finish our jobs first. We can make no definite plans, we go where information is. So will we be at Alice Springs having a rest? Will we be in the Tanami Desert, where I want to see the remarkable work wildlife scientists are doing there in co-operation with Aborigines? Will we be somewhere east of the Alice at a ruby field that alarmed all the Australian colonies in 1888 when Darwin Chinese advertised for a guide to lead 500 miners there? Or will we be somewhere to the north at a wolfram field where the Australian government put 600 Chinese to work in the 1940s? They had come in as refugees from islands overrun by Japanese, and the White Australia government, to whom the word Chinese meant coolies, put them all to work.

Elaine's great-grandfather, John Melville, spent Christmas of 1855 in the Northern Territory. He was camped on the Victoria River with A. C. Gregory's north Australian expedition. Christmas Day went unnoticed. New Year's Day was unintentionally lively. Gregory was about to set out on an inland exploration. The party had thirty packhorses loaded with five months' provisions, six saddle-horses ready to be mounted. In a salute to the day and the beginning of the expedition, the captain of the *Tom Tough*, the accompanying schooner, fired his cannon. John Melville left a brief account in manuscript. 'All the horses were frightened and ran away with all the provisions and scattered in every direction and it took nearly a week to find them all and then they were minus some of the saddles and some of the provisions.'

So this year I will miss what has become our traditional Christmas dinner: iced cherry soup which is mostly deep red cherries and red wine, a ham cured superbly by Brian Sheppard of Gunnedah baked in a double wrapping of foil in our slow-combustion stove, home-grown chickens steamed in wine and set in a lightly curried cream sauce, a salad of whatever is freshest, old Hunter whites from Lindeman's, then brandy sauce and suet pudding spiked with old silver coins. Joan treasured them and always swapped them back for metric coins. Sometimes we thought of clingstone peaches instead of pudding, but we always rejected the idea.

It is too soon yet for me to be used to Christmases without Joan. Elaine's husband died seventeen years ago but it will be her first Christmas away from her tall good-looking family. Wherever we will be, we will enjoy Christmas together without a Leichhardt-like commitment to enjoy it. Both of us take our work seriously, but neither of us takes ourselves seriously enough to interfere with good living.

*No one advocating
more uranium mining
in Kakadu is impartial*

Suppose the first storm of the season washes a handful of sandy soil into a clear spring-fed pool at the head of Jim Jim Creek in Kakadu National Park. The fresh chemicals cause a little bloom of algae that a young Black Bream eats. A few days later a Water Monitor makes a snatch at the little fish and chops off the end of its tail. The injured fish can live in quiet water but it has no power to resist the first flood of the pre-wet. It washes over waterfalls and through lagoons down into the tidal reaches of the South Alligator River where a fast ebb picks it up and carries it to the estuary. A Little Black Cormorant, beating up from Barron Island, dives on it as it floats helplessly on the surface and then, by coincidence, flies up for a few days' quiet fishing in the same mountain pool that the fish lived in. After several dives in the cold water, the cormorant perches on a bare limb, spreads its wings to let the warm sun in and excretes on the same ground the handful of soil washed off. So it returned what was taken, perhaps with interest.

When another storm washes the droppings into the pool, they might go through a process so complicated it will take a hundred years to return. The cycling of nutrients in a river system, the vital assembly of an entire unexploited valley and associated uplands has never been studied. In asking for the Stage 2 extension of Kakadu as a World Heritage Listing and for the pastoral leases Gimbat and Goodparla as national park, scientists are not being greedy. They are asking for the opportunity to make essential studies that can be made nowhere else.

We arrived in Darwin in the middle of the universal row over the listing of Stage 2. We saw a film made by the Northern Territory government in which Harry Butler and Professor Mellanby made fools of themselves for money. 'It is second rate, that's what it is,' said Harry Butler. Professor Mellanby had just driven across one of the world's busiest areas of wildlife but, instead of recognising it, he regretted the lions, antelopes, wildebeest and elephants he would have seen in East Africa. 'In a very much longer drive through Kakadu Stage 2, you are lucky to see a couple of kangaroos and an emu,' he said. To get good examples of buffalo damage Harry Butler had to direct the cameraman to a securely fenced paddock of 30,000 hectares where 2300 buffaloes are run so that the damage they do can be compared with an adjacent area that they are fenced out of. The film asserted that the majority of the area was not worth a world listing. The unstated implication was that mining would do it no harm.

I do not agree that there should be a blanket restriction on mining in all parks. Some mining in some parks, as some timber milling in some parks, might be harmless. A decision needs to be made for each area by impartial scientists. No one advocating more uranium mining in Kakadu is impartial. All have calculated their percentages of billions of dollars.

Uranium is frightening. Nothing else has the power in one catastrophe to poison a region for thousands of years. Certainly Kakadu has lived with uranium for many thousands of years. An Aboriginal trade route ran through the area where the Ranger mine is now. Regular runners developed sores on their legs that would not heal. Magela Creek that drains the area shows a higher than normal count of uranium. So do all the animals that live in its waters. But it is a safe count as hundreds of generations of healthy Aborigines that hunt there bear witness. The plentiful run-off dilutes the uranium and it flows harmlessly into the ocean when floods wash over natural levees.

The rich, wide creek supplies file snakes, Water Monitors, Magpie Geese, mussels, ducks, Black Bream, barramundi, turtles. The banks supply wild fruit. It is vital that Aborigines continue to hunt there. They make little success of hunting in supermarkets. Although they have mostly accommodated to a white modern age, they have not learnt to select white food.

Accidental spills of tailings water have frightened them. In a report to the House of Representatives Standing Committee the Northern Land Council referred to the 'gross carelessness' of the company operating Ranger. Since 1981 there have been sixteen breaks in the tailings pipelines, terrifying calamities although they did no harm. According to local stories the four holes in the pipe flanges did not always match so the company made do with two bolts and two G-clamps which broke under pressure. The Minister for Mines and Energy forced the company to replace the pipeline.

But now there is also a new pipeline from Retention Pond 2 to Magela Creek. Rather outlandishly, the Department of Mines and Energy recommended the approval of the pipeline with the injunction that approval was not permission to use. Could somebody in error open the gate valve? Would a change in Federal Government lift the floodgate?

To those managing Kakadu the company is a group of schoolboys practising baseball with a box of rusty hand grenades as balls. And too many fear that all the OSS, the Office of the Supervising Scientist, can do from its tormented position as umpire is to call out, 'Don't hit so hard, Johnny! Don't hit so hard!'

They are aware that Kakadu is the most important park in Australia

At the headquarters of Kakadu National Park a wide window forms one side of a cage that houses Louie I and Louie II, two orphaned curlews. Louie senior, who had a wing amputated after being hit by a car, roams the grounds. About 2 a.m. each morning he stands under the bedroom windows and howls. The Stone Curlew, almost exterminated in the south by ploughs and trampling sheep, is still plentiful in the north.

Dr A. J. Press told us about the park and arranged for Wendy Murray to show us Aboriginal paintings. It is a delight to talk to the staff at Kakadu. One expects knowledge but meets enthusiasm also. They are aware that Kakadu is the most important park in Australia.

It is important for what is not there. There are no rabbits, no hares, no foxes, no starlings, sparrows, house mice, Black Rats nor the bitter little Mosquito Fish: vermin that disorder almost every other Australian park. There is no unnatural growth of timber. Trees grow in much the same density and in much the same dominance as they have for hundreds of years. In almost every other park the stands of timber are 100 to 300 times thicker than they were at the time of white settlement. There is little change in the original grasses. Over most of Australia the best grasses were trampled out within six years of being stocked with sheep and cattle.

There are very few feral honey bees that interfere with native bees and disorganise the pollination of many plants, there are very few goats, few cats. There are pigs which are increasing and have

Dingoes, exceptionally big and healthy . . .

to be eradicated. There is mimosa, one of the few exotic plants. Brought in from south-east Asia about 1890, it seemed to be harmless until it suddenly took over land bared by buffaloes in the 1970s. A vigorous, thorny, fast-growing legume, it could take over the park. Four hardworking staff keep it in check but their job will never be done because of the outside infestations. There are buffaloes, extraordinarily successful animals that built up from a few dozen imported from Timor in the 1820s and 1830s by the three aborted British military settlements. By 1845, when Ludwig Leichhardt came through, they numbered hundreds: 'buffalo tracks spread in every direction, particularly down the creeks'. In 100 years of skin-getting, shooting for pet meat and now catching and taming for live export, about 700,000 have been taken. They turned superb lily lagoons into muddy wallows, they pugged up monsoon forests and delicate trees died, they pushed over palms for the attractive cabbage, they devastated grasslands, they knocked down natural levees and allowed salt water into freshwater paperbark swamps, their tracks started gully erosion on creeks and rivers. They damaged Kakadu severely but most of them have now been captured and the land has responded as no one thought it could. In only five years it has almost effaced their presence, not by disordered growth but by replacing what was there in the original order.

Kakadu National Park is very important for what is there. Dingoes, exceptionally big and healthy, keep the Agile Wallabies in control. In New South Wales and Victoria kangaroos no longer have any natural predators. They build up in parks to unsupportable numbers, then crash with disease. We heard a pack of Dingoes howling in mid-afternoon. We saw several walking about, wary but confident. In the Northern Territory there are no wool growers to put a price on their scalps.

The galleries of rock paintings record life from 30,000 years ago to modern times. Wendy showed us those at Nourlangie, a wondrous place. Huge slabs of hard, sandstone conglomerate stand tier on tier. In one place a spring trickles out about forty metres up and starts a little creek. We drank the water, cool, peaty and delicious. In the 1960s Najombolmi, Barramundi Charlie, a rare artist, retouched ancient figures and interpreted myths in new paintings.

Elaine and I travelled on a barge round Yellow Water Lagoon. Phil Burt, the boatman, enjoys his work, too. We saw three of the eighty-four crocodiles poke their noses out to breathe then submerge below streams of bubbles. A Great-billed Heron, a rare bird, stepped quickly up the bank and half hid behind a tree. We ate wild passionfruit that trailed along the bank. A white-breasted Sea Eagle attacked an immature Wedge-tail. A big Whaler Shark cruised by. It had been locked in fresh water for at least six months.

In its extended form, Kakadu National Park would be 2,000,000 hectares of extraordinarily complex landscape: of spectacular escarpments winding around for 200 kilometres on the eastern and southern boundaries, of seashore and mangrove swamps, of rivers and creeks, lagoons and rock pools, monsoon forest, dry forest and grassland, of flood plains and uplands. It houses every plant and animal that were there 200 years ago: 1400 species of plants, many of them beautiful, many undescribed; 10,000 species of insects, including the big, red and blue Leichhardt Grasshopper; birds and mammals in plenty, some of them found nowhere else. The commonest bird in the park, the magnificent Magpie Goose, depends on it for its existence. During the dry 2,500,000 flock to its lagoons. That is seventy per cent of the total number of birds.

In its final form, Kakadu National Park would be the most important park in the world.

. . . the remarkable recovery
of the country
is being watched
by keen eyes . . .

Some of the best of Australia's scientists are studying Kakadu National Park as few parks have ever been studied. At Kapalga, a core within that park to which the public is not admitted, CSIRO scientists have been studying 70,000 hectares at extreme level since 1975. Dr Richard Brathwaite took us in there. He was the first to do extensive work on the rich lowland forests and flood plains. We had arrived at a fortunate time. Dick was performing for Rae Allen of the ABC so he had run his live-catching traps out of schedule. Rae wanted to produce a TV documentary to counter Harry Butler's controversial video.

Kapalga stretches from the Arnhem Highway to the sea between the West and South Alligator Rivers. The northern section of 30,000 hectares is fenced off to run buffaloes. They have been excluded from the southern section of 40,000 hectares, and the remarkable recovery of the country is being watched by keen eyes of many disciplines.

One area of forty-five hectares running down from stony slopes across a creek is trapped regularly and thoroughly. Traps are set out on three nights a month, 360 of them twenty-five metres apart, measured by tape, in twelve lines fifty metres apart, run by compass. Every site is marked by a permanent numbered peg. Each mammal caught is identified, located, weighed, measured, sexed, then released. Almost every mammal in the ten species there has been caught at least once, some of them again and again.

The Northern Brown Bandicoot behaves wildly on a first catching, tearing at the research worker with sharp hind claws. But after many baits and many nights in traps, they wait patiently for release and seem to enjoy being stroked before they move off. They have a gestation of twelve and a half days, the shortest period of all mammals.

A Pale Field-rat, the commonest catch, has been known to turn and leap at the face of the man who released it. They keep dry during the wet by tunnelling into termite mounds. Other species of termites and several species of ants use these mounds, too, as well as nesting birds. After a few seasons as a rat warren the mounds collapse. Then the bandicoots build grass nests on top and kick ant bed over them to harden as a roof. Snakes and lizards use the holes. Just as in Glebe, said Elaine, first there are the well-maintained cottages owned or rented, then come the squatters as they deteriorate, then the slimy developers.

Dick put out sixty traps only and caught thirty animals, an astonishing catch that confirms the richness of the area. The most interesting were two Delicate Mice, tiny uncommon creatures with rust-coloured flanks, so frail that if you handle them carelessly they die.

Dr Laurie Corbett, who has worked on wild dogs all round the world, can state confidently that there are about twenty wild cats and sixty Dingoes in Kapalga. He is certain that Dingoes did not come to Australia with Aborigines but with Asian people who carried them aboard ship as pets and as food. And some Dingoes made the return journey thousands of years ago. There is a louse on dogs throughout Asia that originated on kangaroos.

On the banks of the South Alligator River there are fossilised shells of big crayfish among roots of mangroves that died 6000 years ago when the seas stopped rising. Packed with the silt that preserved them, the cast-off shells sit in the mud at low tide with bright blue claws held out in front, blue tails curled under. They look like dormant live things in wait for a special tide that will revive them.

The lagoons in the southern section have revived. Tall lilies and short lilies mass over them with blue, yellow, white and red flowers. Crocodiles shelter among them and sometimes launch themselves at a swimming Magpie Goose. Hundreds of different birds work the banks, the shallows, the deeper open water. Lotus Birds with exceptionally long toes to spread their weight walk on top of the floating leaves. If danger threatens, the males clamp eggs or young under their wings and run to safety.

An outlandish plant, *Amorphophallus glabra*, has revived too. It sends up narrow, pointed, mottled green stems that leaves break out of, then, out of the ground near them, a bigger mottled flower bract that opens out into a frilled, purple-green disc about thirty-five centimetres across with a big, red, glans-like head in the centre. It smells like rotten meat. Flies and dung beetles flock to it.

It is one of the few plants that grow as understorey in the densely canopied monsoon forests. And these lovely places are also recovering. They grow where the water table is always near the surface. Since most of them are only a hectare or two in area, they are at risk from fire, wind and buffaloes. Aborigines protected them. They valued them for the yams that once grew in the understorey, and for several native fruits including the pleasant, tart Red Apples and the figs of the banyan that sends down aerial roots from its branches. Some of the roots become trunks that branch again, and the one tree grows into colonnades of trees.

Kapalga, the whole of Kakadu, teems with life. And the scientists know that all they know now is little more than a base for deeper studies.

The summer
is the best time
to come to Darwin

Two exotic sounds distinguish Darwin: the helicopter buzz of overhead fans and the staccato chirp of Asian House Geckoes. Every household turns its fans on in every room when the humidity rises in mid-September, turns them off about mid-May. If the air is not kept stirring, blue mould paints walls and ceilings. Unlike the native House Geckoes in the south, the northern geckoes are active all year. They cluster round verandah lights and call from house to house, from house to garden trees.

We came to Darwin for a fortnight, we stayed for five weeks. We did not merely see Darwin, we lived in it, first with Peter and Sheila Forrest, then with Lill Smith and Phil Gerner. Peter is a writer and broadcaster with a deep knowledge of Northern Territory history, Sheila is in charge of the Northern Territory Reference Library. Lill is an imaginative screen printer. Phil is an engineer working now at Tipperary about 200 kilometres south and helping to turn it from several run-down cattle stations into a complex costing tens of millions that will run 200,000 cattle and perhaps buffaloes on improved pastures. So they opened unexpected and exciting doors for us on the work we came here to do.

Darwin is a beautiful city. Gardens are full of palms, and mangoes, and trees with huge leaves. The spectacular Elephant Ear Acacia bloomed for us. Fuzzy balls of light yellow flowers over two centimetres across weigh down branches of grey-green, half-moon phyllodes. Flying foxes and householders wait for the mangoes to soften on the trees. Too often the flying foxes cannot wait.

They clutch at too-hard fruit with their wing hooks, take a few bites out of them, then drop them on the ground. Possums pick them up, carry them to their favourite dining spot on path or lawn, and chew and suck till the big seeds are covered with nothing but yellow fibre.

Grasshoppers ten centimetres long fly about the gardens, and delicate Red-headed Honeyeaters that are not a millimetre longer. Occasionally one sees a Crimson Finch more like a jewel than a bird. Each flowering tree is noisy with Rainbow Lorikeets. Black and white Torres Strait Pigeons make their untidy nests in parks. Lill has a Frilled Lizard that lives in one corner of her garden. It goes for fast, two-legged runs on a neighbouring school oval, and stops to rear higher and flare its cheek pieces if something surprises it. Everywhere there are Green Ants with amber thoraxes and light green abdomens. They build tree nests by stitching leaves together, sometimes using chains of ants to pull in leaves eight centimetres away. As the distance shortens, end links drop off. Aborigines used these ants as a condiment. When eating kangaroo flesh they squeezed the lemony contents of the abdomens into their mouths.

The summer is the best time to come to Darwin. Most of the tourists are dodging the sultry weather, unjustly said to be unbearable. 'What will the temperature be in Darwin tomorrow?' 'Thirty-two degrees Centigrade.' 'What was the temperature three months ago?' 'Thirty-two degrees Centigrade.' It is rare for the temperature to reach 35°. Only the humidity varies much between the wet and the dry. And nearly always there is a breeze to counter the humidity.

So when Elaine and I went to Doctors Gully to see the fish fed, we did not have to look over the shoulders of 600 tourists. A little girl sat alone in the shallow water on a cement ramp feeding bread to Diamond-scaled Mullet. She had fish in her lap, fish all round her, opening their lips and demanding. A couple of hundred, thirty to forty centimetres long, swam about waiting their turn. Each high tide about twenty species come in to be fed. Each group behaves differently. The mullet are the quietest. Very big Milkfish cruise about quickly on the surface and leap for the big pieces.

Diamond Fish with yellow-tipped scales cruise under them and flash up for the crumbs. A Silver Gull and a Turnstone patrolled the cement platform. The Turnstone was avoiding a Siberian winter.

Each half hour from 1 a.m. to 4 a.m. during holidays the Drunks' Flights take off from Darwin Airport to reach southern cities just after the night curfews end. People go to parties, then to the airport bar to wait. They are noisy and happy gatherings. Airport announcers join in like sideshow spruikers. 'Announcing the arrival of Flight 223 from Alice Springs, folks. Just settling down on the runway now. Prepare to go aboard for the big flight south.'

The old Australian attitude that the happiest time in Darwin is when one is leaving has almost disappeared. But the most stable population, and the oldest money, are still Chinese.

Darwin is the least racist city in the world. It is relaxed and happy. Everybody talks to everybody. 'You'll be back! You'll be back!' people told us as we left.

*Despite a hundred years
of fervid White Australia,
Darwin is
cosmopolitan Asian*

A white Australian in shorts and thongs walks along Darwin's mall with a naked Aboriginal child on his shoulders. The child's sweat mixes with his own and runs in gutters down his dirty back. No one sees him as unusual. A white girl stands on a street corner talking fluently to an Aboriginal man in his own language. The former leader of the Opposition, Bob Collins, is married to a Tiwi woman from Bathurst Island. Darwin's lord mayor is Chinese. Business is dominated by Greeks, financial security by Chinese. There are Italians, Indonesians, Malaysians, Sinhalese, Hindus, Danes, Swedes, Scots, English, French, New Zealanders, Americans, Japanese, Vietnamese, Thais, Timorese, Tamils. Ask a child, 'How many races go to your school?' and the answer is, 'It would be easier to name those who don't.' Despite a hundred years of fervid White Australia, Darwin is cosmopolitan Asian.

Each Saturday morning a market in Parap Square sells superb Asian fruit: breadfruit, jackfruit, soursops, star fruit, star apples, guavas, custard apples, bitter melons, Chinese cabbages, pawpaw flowers for Indonesian cookery, real tomatoes, not the armour-plated imitations sold in the south. 'Are these grown in big gardens or backyards?' I asked the girl with red pawpaws for sale. 'Backyards,' she said. 'Europeans don't worry. They grow a bit for their own use. Asians work. Make money.' Small, sweet pineapples are peeled thinly, then three eyes at a time are cut out in slanted Vs. The top is chopped off about six centimetres long. The result is a spiral of pineapple with a handle.

All cooked food is superbly fresh. Chicken wings are boned and stuffed with prawns. Spicy fish and pork is presented in cleverly folded banana-leaf dishes. Balls of translucent sticky rice are stuffed with dates and rolled in long threads of coconut.

European restaurants are second-rate. Preposterously, they still offer garlic bread, they overdo the garnishings. Malaysian and Chinese restaurants are good. The Bagus Indonesian restaurant is superb. On Sundays the proprietor's two young sons, one nine years old, one thirteen, act as waiters. Notably good-looking children, they serve with amiable gravity. Their mother is chef. Entrée is trepang, the subtly flavoured dried sea-slug that formed the first article of trade between Australia and China. For at least two hundred years before white settlement, Macassan prahus, some of them owned by Chinese merchants, sailed down on the wet monsoon, sailed back on the change.

All through the last quarter of the nineteenth century, Chinese fishermen wet pickled and dried most of their catch for export to China but always offered fresh fish on the local market. No one sells fresh fish any more. 'We've got fresh frozen,' shopkeepers say happily, indicating nasty, frosty, plastic packages of stiff fillets. Fishing boats have got bigger, close catches smaller. Boats go out for weeks at a time. Fish has to be frozen. But whole fish can be frozen so that they do not lose too much of their identity. Even Sydney rock oysters come up frozen in the shells, an absurdity. Oysters keep for two or three weeks in hessian bags in the shade. Cobb & Co. carted hundreds of bags in the 1860s, 1870s and 1880s. Hotels in far western New South Wales had cellars to put them in, or better still, airy spaces under floorboards.

The limiting factor of what Darwin can do is its population, still only 60,000. So the collection at its reference library astonishes, as does its museum, both fit for a population of a million or more. There is a fine collection of preserved Northern Territory animals, presented imaginatively in the museum, and an especially good art gallery with Fred Williams, Margaret Preston, three of the best of Arthur Boyd, John Olsen, Drysdale, a wide range of old and modern works, displayed beautifully.

Nothing is crowded. Even small works are highlighted by their placing. The Aboriginal gallery is remarkable. One sees too many bark paintings of scratchy lizards and malformed kangaroos. Tiwi artists from Melville and Bathurst Islands are conscious of every stroke as artists ought to be. Figures move, or fit patterns.

Darwin's police force is outstanding, efficient and unusually courteous. A recent edition of the *Northern Territory News* carried a big apology to the Malak Primary School from the Northern Territory police. They had incorrectly told a reporter that a pupil was growing marijuana in the school grounds. It was an ex-pupil who was sneaking in to water one plant.

The Northern Territory has not the government it deserves. Too many of its politicians are old-fashioned, quarrelsome and dubious. No rural ventures have ever prospered. Rice, cattle, sugar cane were tried in the wrong places, at the wrong time, with the wrong stocks by the wrong people. Buffalo, new breeds of cattle, might rejuvenate the stock industry. Crocodile farming might be successful. People are experimenting with many tropical fruits. Some are planting too many hectares.

As capital, the beautiful city of Darwin is still part way through a dream.

Kangaroos lope among symbols,
turtles spread into space

Lill Smith takes a spoonful of jellied paint and runs it in an even line along the top of a tightly stretched silk-screen. She might put a blob or two or other colours somewhere along it. The movement looks haphazard but she has placed the right amount in the exact position to fade one colour into the next. Then she makes a quick sweep with a board that forces paint through the screen, through the pattern under it, onto the cloth she is working on. She lifts the arm of the spider holding that screen, swings it away, and clamps down the next screen as it comes into position to print the next colour.

Lill prints T-shirts to order for profit, she makes intricate designs on sarongs and materials for her friends. She has so many friends she seldom sells any lengths of cloth. Her extraordinary vitality prints itself all around Darwin. Her partner, Phil Gerner, and Elaine and I intended taking her to the Latin Tavern for her birthday dinner, but so many called in with greetings and bottles and food and stayed on, we did not get there until the next night. Luigi, the proprietor, hugged her as she entered and conducted her proudly to a table where a bottle of champagne waited on ice. None of us had mentioned her birthday to him. People repay Lill with unexpected delights.

She lives almost in the heart of the city and pedals in on a bicycle. 'I was in that little underwear shop today and Alec Fong Lim, the mayor, came in,' she told us. 'He's just back from a massive heart operation in Adelaide. The owner of the shop hugged him. "Alec, you're looking well again," she called. He wanted underwear for his wife. "Thirty years we've been married," he explained, "and I've never bought her underwear. I need help." '

'Where else,' asked Lill, 'would a shop full of people learn that the wife of the mayor of a capital city takes a size 12 top and a size 14 bottom?' I took out paper and pen to make a note. 'Dimension it! Dimension it!' cried Lill, who puns brilliantly. 'You can't use that.'

'Why not? It shows why the mayor is so popular. And you.'

The end process of silk-screening is setting the colours with heat. Annie, a Chinese friend of Lill's, comes in to iron the T-shirts. Slight and animated, she pronounces English as though it derives from the Orient. She once backed a racehorse named Mr Ping because Lill's 'ping hibisket' (pink hibiscus) was in full flower the day he was running. The horse won at good odds. Buddha, to whom she offers a cup of fragrant tea each morning before she pours her own, laughed as he oversaw her betting.

Annie began work in Malaysia when she was seven years old. 'I little child, my mother sick, too sick. She gave me to a friend. She treat me as a buffalo. All day I work, work, work. Make cigarette. One day make one thousand cigarette, one day two thousand, three thousand. Forty girl, big room, by hand. Tobacco, like that, roll, roll, roll. Then the boss, the bastard, he come feel them, no lumps, no empty here. Carry tin, on bike, only a kid, fourteen, carry tin. On back seventy kilo, in front thirty kilo, no put in front, bike rear up like this.' A convoy of children carted black tin ore thirty kilometres along a narrow mountain track from mine to bagging shed by the sea.

Naomi Briston, a beautiful Aboriginal girl, came to learn silk-screening. Annie scorns Aborigines as she scorns anyone without a natural work ethic. Lill introduced them. 'She's *coloured*, Lill!' said Annie as though Naomi could not hear her. Then she altered the accent accusingly, '*She's* coloured!'

'Yes, I know, Annie, I know!' said Lill. 'Naomi's black.'

'She coloured, Lill.' Annie sat down, waved her hands in front of her, then let them drop resignedly into her lap.

Naomi has poise to go with her beauty. She was unconcerned. And once Annie saw the quality of the designs Naomi was making her opinion changed. Kangaroos lope among symbols, turtles spread into space.

Her father is part Filipino so he was snatched away from his parents when he was young and sent to a mission on Bathurst Island in the savage Australian campaign to Christianise all mixed-race children. Naomi speaks some Filipino, some Tiwi and her mother's Aboriginal language as well as English. She mostly lives an urban life but enjoys fishing and hunting for food. 'The long-necked turtles out of the river are delicious,' she told me. 'Lie them on their backs on coals and the shell holds all the juices as they cook.' She fishes for barramundi at Bathurst Island. 'There are plenty there. We pull in fish after fish. And sometimes we catch a dugong. They cry like babies when the harpoon goes in.' She consciously switches away from their cries and their grotesquely human appearance and thinks of cooking the superb flesh.

When we left her, Lill was experimenting with designs using Mimi women, the thin female figures of Aboriginal cave paintings. 'They're so active, so graceful,' she said. Lill will take them off the rocks and let them run around Darwin, and wherever else her shirts go.

*Dozens died on the track
or in their hasty camps
of bamboo, paperbark
and grass*

W e spent Christmas and New Year at Pine Creek, south of Darwin. Elaine cooked a Northern Territory Christmas dinner: iced watermelon soup which is mostly melon and Rhine Riesling, roast fillet of buffalo marinated in red wine and served with snowpeas and asparagus, then mangoes and cream sharpened with chilli and tamarind. We drank a vintage champagne with enough years in it to make it superb, and a good Australian red that I decanted into a washed-out plastic drink container. One has to leave the crystal behind on a camping trip.

For the hundreds of Chinese gold-diggers who came to Pine Creek in the late 1870s, food was a matter of urgent and difficult logistics. There were no wagons for sale. Horses were scarce and inordinately dear. So for the first two or three years incoming Chinese walked 130 kilometres from the old town of Southport at the head of Port Darwin and carried their food and equipment with them on shoulder poles. They ate 700 grams of rice a day each, they needed at least four weeks' supply until they could be sure of getting more in. They could carry fifty kilograms comfortably so forty per cent of the weight of what was needed to work a new goldfield in a new country was rice. They had dried fish and salt cabbage to add flavour to the rice but no fresh vegetables until their gardeners had time to grow them. Since they carried polished rice, a strange preference of Chinese even today, they went through a period of two or three months without any vitamin B to protect them from beri-beri. Dozens died on the track or in their hasty camps of bamboo, paperbark and grass. Their feet swelled, their legs blackened, their hearts failed in hours or days. They recognised some of the symptoms of beri-beri but they had never known it to strike so suddenly. They called it The Australian Disease.

During the building of the Darwin–Pine Creek railway between 1887 and 1889, Millar Brothers, the contractors, engaged Dr Stow to care for their European, Chinese and Tamil employees at twopence per head per working day. It was the first medical scheme in Australia. Since the number employed was always more than 1400, Stow had the opportunity to make enormous money, over $7000 a year when the fat salary of the government resident was $3000. But Stow was both lazy and greedy. He sublet much of the work to Dr H. H. Bovill, who was in charge of the government hospital at Burrundie, a field to the north of Pine Creek, and spent weeks at a time in Darwin. There he came to a comfortable arrangement with Dr Percy Moore Wood, the medical officer, to supply the drugs free that he was supposed to buy out of his contract money. In addition, Bovill admitted his subcontracted patients to the Burrundie hospital at government expense.

The government resident reported what was going on to the South Australian minister controlling the Territory. No word of the scandal ever reached a newspaper, no charge was brought against the doctors, but all three made a sudden departure from the Territory.

More and more Chinese came in to the goldfields. When numbers reached 6000, they outnumbered Europeans about five to one. For several years Chinese controlled all the fields. Under expert miners and businessmen like Pin Que, described as the whitest man in the Territory, they bought batteries and worked reefs successfully, the only place in Australia where the Chinese engaged in reef mining.

On all the old fields there is still evidence of how they lived and worked, a little shrine where a god sat and looked down on a curving creek, stone-pitched dams, aqueducts, stone ovens, stone retorts for smelting gold. There are few remains of the insubstantial houses that they built of whatever was nearest them but in one place we found rectangular stone platforms built to keep their beds out of the water flowing down a hillside during the wet. Piles of gravelly mullock run in strips broad and narrow over thousands of square kilometres. Often one can still see the form of the shallow shafts they dug, little squares or rectangles that just gave room for a small man to bend over. When he struck a vein of gold the Chinese digger cut in along it as economically as a rabbit, and threw the dirt behind him. He sought pay dirt, not comfort.

At Pine Creek new mining companies are harvesting the deep gold the Chinese left behind. The teeth of open-cut machinery tear at the earth, feeding on both gold and dross so as to miss nothing. Their appetite is inexhaustible. They feed twenty-four hours a day, 365 days a year.

*At Pine Creek
one drives
out of the Australia
that southerners know*

At Pine Creek the country changes from unfamiliar but identifiable dry-country growth to exotic-looking tropical growth. Leaves broaden remarkably, dispense with waxy coatings and hold themselves flat to the steaming sunlight. In open forests of marvellous shrubs I recognised nothing except the pandanus and palms I have read about. To the Chinese miners moving south the country would not have looked nearly as foreign as it did to us moving north. At Pine Creek one drives out of the Australia that southerners know.

Wild buffaloes roam there in astonishing numbers. One sees them whenever one drives off the highway. Where cattle are undersized and poor, the buffaloes are broad, sleek and fat. They have a tropic authority. They walk as though they were made for the country, young bulls together, cows and calves in a separate mob, cast-out bulls alone and dangerous. In the middle of the day they lie in waterholes often with no more than their nostrils above water. From a distance they are almost indistinguishable from crocodiles until one raises its head to see what is intruding instead of avoiding it by sinking under a stream of bubbles.

All native animals are still intact in the north. The rare and beautiful Hooded Parrot with a broad yellow shoulder slash against an emerald breast is common at Pine Creek. We could not find one anywhere, though a small flock had been feeding in the grounds of the school for weeks before we arrived. The female nests in a tall termite mound and the male stands guard on top. The termites seal off the damage made with beak and claws and leave a dry nesting chamber that maintains a constant temperature. Chinese miners dug out chambers in these mounds, too, and stored their dynamite in them. They closed the narrow entrances with paperbark.

We stayed at Pine Creek in demountable units with an extraordinarily well-equipped kitchen attached. Lance Lawrence and his French wife, Sylvie, are building up a motel, store and fuel depot. The new mining is increasing the population of the town quickly, from 100 a couple of years ago to an expected 2000 this year. Lance and Sylvie also own a mango orchard in a beautiful valley flanked by granite walls. A creek flows through it, fed by several springs. Chinese gardeners, attracted by the permanent water, began to cultivate it last century and, under different owners, continued until after the last war when they sold vegetables by the truck load to the Australian army. They terraced the whole valley so that the springs flooded it naturally. Mangoes that they planted 100 years ago still grow along the creek and still yield good crops. Self-sown guavas and custard apples perpetuate equally old species. Here and there taro grows or a yam climbs a tree.

Lance took us out to see the orchard. His sister, Gaye, lives there. She has Red-backed Wrens in her house garden, studies in black and crimson as beautiful as the Superb Blue Wrens in our own garden. Crimson Finches nest under her verandah. One pair flew in through louvres and built a nest in a toilet bag hanging just above a washbasin that several people use several times a day.

Animals in the sparsely settled north behave with the same innocence as animals in southern Australia 150 years ago. Native Cats kill fowls and steal eggs as enthusiastically as they did before they were eradicated in New South Wales and Victoria. 'You just can't live with them,' miners and landowners told us. 'They'll rip their way into a tent, open a tuckerbox and eat everything in it. They break into workshops, chew up rubber, plastic tubing, insulation tape and shit all over everything they can't destroy.' They have been known to enter kitchens and tear open cans of food. At Kakadu one raced through a picnic party sitting round a fire and snatched a sausage frying in a pan. Another levered its way through a window at National Park Headquarters and ate a big collection of preserved frogs that a scientist had made over several weeks. The formalin affected it and it was staggering drunkenly around the laboratory the next morning.

One of the marvels of the north is the fishing. On New Year's Day Lance took us to the headwaters of the Mary River to fish for barramundi. The stream is narrow there, the pools short and the banks overgrown. One needs a short whippy rod to drop the line under leaves and spider webs into bed-sized patches of water. Lance is expert, he worked the water for seven or eight kilometres upstream and came back with two good fish. Elaine and I tried our lures downstream with no luck so then we fished with worms to catch live bait fish. Good-sized Eel-tailed Catfish bit instead. I used to catch these fine fish in the Namoi and the Barwon but European Carp have almost eradicated them.

Lance cooked the barramundi that night. We had never eaten it fresh out of the water and it was a superb beginning to the New Year. And it means we have to go back while the taste is still with us to catch our own barramundi.

*His words
carry Aboriginal imagery
in musical Chinese tones*

Johnny Pangquee speaks beautifully. He is one quarter Aboriginal and three-quarters Chinese. His words carry Aboriginal imagery in musical Chinese tones. Elaine and I spoke to him on his farm on the outskirts of Darwin. Horses thrive there and a big flock of goats and a pet Magpie Goose that feeds with the bantams and Guinea fowl and laying hens.

Johnny's grandfather was Pin Que, the leading miner in the Northern Territory from the mid-1870s to 1886. He pegged four claims on the Union Reef north of Pine Creek, employed up to forty men, worked down to heavy water at eighty metres, and made good profit from stone yielding thirty grams to the tonne. European miners insisted that nothing less than sixty grams could be made to pay. When water failed at the battery that served several reefs, as it usually did during the dry, Pin Que continued mining and put his ore down to grass until the wet. He hand dollied any rich stone for working expenses. Women in China still use the same implement for grinding rice flour: a steel-shod pole about a metre long pounded up and down in a short metal cylinder.

Pin Que spoke excellent English and had probably gained his mining expertise in Victoria. Certainly when the government resident asked him to go to Singapore to engage experienced miners, he replied that he could get much better men from Victoria. Alfred Giles, who managed Springvale, one of the earliest cattle stations in the Territory, often mentions him in his diaries. If Giles needed a cook, he telegraphed Pin Que. If Pin Que needed bullocks for the butcher shop and store he ran as a sideline, he telegraphed Giles. That store cost him a lot of money one wet year. He engaged carriers to bring up six months' supply from Southport at $180 a tonne, enormous rates for those days, though the horses could manage only three kilometres a day through the bogs. After several weeks on the track, the teamsters came to a river too high in flood to cross. They unloaded the stores and returned. The river rose higher and swept the stores away.

Pin Que died in May 1886. No one knows what he died of. Dysentery, malaria, tuberculosis and beri-beri were the chief killers of those days. But before he died he went home to his wife and family in China and brought back his son, who became equally well known as Jimmy Pan Quee. He made the first alteration to the transliteration of the name.

The reefs at the Union cut out. The name Pin Que went out of the mining records. Jimmy Pan Quee worked a copper mine on the Daly River in conjunction with Willy Lee. He married a half-Chinese girl, Kitty, who lived with the local Aboriginal tribe. Elaine and I hoped to talk to her. 'She's old, oh she's eighty-six,' said Johnny, 'and she's blind, but she has a beautiful memory.' But she was sick when we went to see her and her memory had failed her. In any case she is unlikely to have been able to answer our questions. Many Chinese men had happy relationships with Aboriginal girls. Life improved immensely for both man and woman. Each learnt new worlds. But language limited what they could tell each other, knowledge was almost unbridgeable. Where was China to a black girl? If her husband was away for weeks, he had gone to Darwin for stores. If he was away for months, 'Maybe he go China.'

Jimmy Pan Quee was known for his humanity, not his business acumen. His name comes into Aboriginal corroborees and into the folksong, 'Down on the Daly River Oh!' that Jim Burgoyne first sang:

> *There was Wallaby George and Charlie Dargie,*
> *Old Skinny Davis and Jimmy Panquee . . .*
> *And where'er you may roam*
> *You will find yourself at home,*
> *They are noted for their hospitality.*

Jimmy Pan Quee lost the copper mine. When he was away in Darwin buying stores someone got Willy Lee so drunk he signed it away. Johnny never knew his father very well. What he most remembers is his repeated statement that he wished he could win the lottery so that he could go home to see his mother. Johnny was snatched away in the awful drive to whiten mixed-race children. 'I was about six and they came and took me. There was a lot of us. They took us to Darwin to the compound at the hospital, girls upstairs, boys downstairs. Then we went to the mission on Bathurst. When we got there we saw all these wild blacks, real myalls they were, and we were frightened. We cried. We were only little fellers.'

If Johnny ever leaves his farm, he will go back to his mother's people, down on the Daly River Oh.

*Too many newcomers
to Darwin bring southern
ideas with them*

The houses of prewar Darwin had galvanised-iron roofs pitched as high as those in the snow country. Without ceilings they gave space for hot air to rise. The galvanised-iron walls were hinged at the top so that they could be pushed outwards with heavy props. Floors were about thirty centimetres off the ground to let the breeze under. The excessively sultry air of the pre-wet is nearly always moving in some direction. If there are sufficient openings one can let it in to blow oneself cool.

Between 1917 and 1920 Chinese carpenters built several tropical houses in the Edith River district north-west of Katherine (pronounced The Kath-er-ine to rhyme with mine even by Darwin ABC). One of them is still standing. Elaine and I drove in to see it after hours spent following misdirections over difficult roads. At last we found John Lee who took us to the old house along boggy farm tracks. Some years ago he lived in it and grew tomatoes that he irrigated from the billabong near it. But mostly he works his earthmoving machinery under contracts that have taken him all over Australia, even to big jobs in Tasmania. Almost eighty years old, he still does long shifts on his bulldozer.

The house is a rectangle of galvanised iron, long, high, and wide, floored with stone. Big sections of the walls push out like awnings. The doorways are nearly two metres wide. The framework is of round White Cypress Pine, immaculately morticed and jointed. The round rafters have been economically sawn lengthways. Within the big living area are two separate bedrooms that one can walk around as if they were huge pieces of furniture. Their lower walls are of bamboo laths, split

An imaginative Chinese builder
used Oriental and English methods . . .
(Photograph by Elaine van Kempen)

on the banks of the Edith River, laced through horizontal wires. Above these walls which are three metres high, a decorative bamboo lattice extends another ninety centimetres. They do not stop any wind that the house welcomes in.

No one knows who built it. An imaginative Chinese builder used Oriental and English methods to produce something wholly different and wholly suitable to the climate.

Too many newcomers to Darwin bring southern ideas with them. A house ought to be a brick box to be warmed in the south, cooled in the north. So they bar the northern monsoon, the southerly buster, the Fremantle doctor and live in artificial atmospheres. A team of young architects in Darwin are designing airy houses under the name of Troppo Architects.

They allow no shelter for rats and cockroaches. Floors are high above ground, shelves and cupboards are open, there are no ceilings. Vented ridges on high roofs act as chimneys for hot air. The reinforcing of every joint defies the cyclones. Slanting screens of metal or fabric, louvres of glass and of metal, fixed, adjustable, of various sizes control wind and rain as much as they can control it. 'It is easy to mop up water,' they say. Fibreboard or light metal walls adjust quickly to changes in temperature. Framework is steel to defy the termites.

'You could now put the frame of this building in the palm of your hand,' wrote one government officer only twelve months after Darwin was established. The South Australian government, scorning the excellent local termite-proof cypress pine, sent up very expensive Jarrah for the first buildings. Most of the Northern Territory's fifty-five species of termites, some of them one and a half centimetres long, found it delicious.

One lovely stone building, the Sue Wah Chin store, survived the war and the several cyclones. Chinese builders in the 1880s used the local porcellanite to put up some fine buildings. For government contracts they took the soft stone from a quarry. For their own work they bored holes in cliff faces at low tide, packed the holes with dried mangrove roots, and when the giant eight-metre tide came in the wood swelled and cracked off slabs of the face.

The Territory Insurance Office is a fine modern building. Constructed of steel and glass, each storey has a wide verandah shaded by metal louvres set out at an angle of forty-five degrees. They suggest the push-out walls of old Darwin.

The jaws clamp
with five-tonne pressure,
the crocodile rolls,
turns . . .

A sure way of maintaining the earth is to domesticate the animals natural to it. The Northern Territory has three crocodile farms that promise success. There is an enthusiastic market for the skins all over the world. Sales for the good flesh will develop.

Elaine and I drove down to the Darwin Crocodile Farm forty kilometres south of the city. John Hannon manages it well. While waiting the five long years for his crop to grow to the marketable length of 1.8 metres, he opened the farm to tourists.

The breeding pool for the salt-water crocodiles covers about four hectares and contains 110 females and twelve males behind a 1.8 metre fence of heavy, linked wire. David Tennyenhuis feeds them three times a week at advertised times. He carries down a basket containing forty-five dead hens, opens a locked gate, places his basket about three metres from the water at the top of a gentle earth ramp and squats beside it. Then he picks up a hen and thumps it on the ground. Immediately crocodiles come to the surface. Perhaps nine or ten swim towards him. Five station themselves half out of the water at the foot of the ramp. The others float behind. They watch one another, heads turning. Eyes assert authority. Then the dominant one rushes. It comes at startling speed, impelled out of the water by a lash of the tail and running high on its legs with mouth wide open. David throws a fowl into its mouth. The jaws clamp with five-tonne pressure, the crocodile rolls, turns, and slides back into the water.

After two years at the farm, David knows the temper of each one. Although others make the same savage charge, he allows them to come right up to him and take the hen out of his hand.

Two crocodiles never come up together. None come without careful checking that it is their turn. After forty are fed, perhaps one or two stragglers come up. That is what the spare fowls are for. What of the other seventy-eight or seventy-nine crocodiles? They were fed two days before, or five. These great creatures, up to four and a half metres long and weighing 750 kilograms, need no more than one fowl a week to keep in prime condition. When they suffer no stress they slow their metabolism till they barely exibit life. A basking crocodile registers a pulse rate of two beats a minute. Its mouth gapes open like that of a stuffed museum specimen. Birds hop up and clean its teeth.

The crocodiles were breeding when we were there. Already fourteen had come out on to the banks to pile and press the old straw put there for them into big mounds. They had dug into them, laid sixty to eighty eggs in spherical piles, covered them up and stood guard. We walked round to see one nest. The female charged, bashed into the netting, then tore at it till she split her lip, so we did not go near any of the others.

The farm workers have to rope them to collect the eggs for incubation. In the wild, the few eggs in the centre of the pile are maintained at 32°C and hatch into males, the majority on the outside, one degree cooler, hatch into females. So the farm incubates the eggs at 31.5°C to get eighty per cent females and twenty per cent males.

The hatchlings are nervous. One man only handles them. Strangers, sudden noises can cause them to fret, stop eating and die. After three months they gain confidence and can be moved 100 at a time into the growing pens where they are fed minced fish with an increasing amount of poultry after they are two years old. The crocodile farm wisely bought a poultry farm next door to keep up the supply of old hens.

They breed freshwater crocodiles, too, in a lovely lily lagoon. And strangely, although the adults are dangerous only at nesting time, the young are much more belligerent than those of the salt-water crocodile. When a keeper walks into their pen, they rise up on their legs, arch their backs and hiss.

The Conservation Commission of the Northern Territory now catches dangerous crocodiles and takes them to the farm instead of shooting them. Miss Piggy attacked boats in the wild. There are tears in the netting one and a half metres off the ground where she has leapt at her keeper. When a big male was put in a pen next to her, she tore down the fence and savaged him.

But now there is Burt, a huge male of similar temperament. He killed three females. So they plan to put him next to Miss Piggy with a stout fence between. They will let them assess one another for a few weeks, then open a gate. Will violence subdue violence, or aggravate it?

*Red earth
and blue-grey spinifex
merge together
to colour the country . . .*

During World War II 600 Chinese men who had been working for the British Phosphate Commission on Nauru and Ocean Island were evacuated to Australia. The government, zealously White Australian, unable to distinguish Chinese from Japanese, and ludicrously afraid of spies, gave them the opportunity of going into a concentration camp or going to work. They chose work. The Manpower Department with absolute power sent them to mine wolfram in central Australia. Tungsten, the metal hardener processed from the ore of wolfram, was in short supply.

The fortunes of wolfram miners depend on war. The black, tin-like metal has been mined off and on at several places in the Northern Territory since 1913. During the last war the mines that used Chinese labour were at Wauchope, south of Tennant Creek (called Waukop in the Territory where spelling and pronunciation are singular), and 120 kilometres east of there at Hatches Creek on the edge of unsettled country marked 'semidesert' on the map. The variable rainfall averages about 300 millimetres.

With detailed maps and expert local advice from Tennant Creek, Elaine and I drove in to the old mining reserve at Hatches Creek. Mauve gravelly plains become the mauve gravelly hills of the Murchison Range. Red earth and blue-grey spinifex merge together to colour the country, but there are broad yellow belts of better grasses and many low trees and shrubs. The hills are the oldest of all hills. Some of them are little more than piles of gravel. Even where rocks maintain their shape, they are so broken they could be taken apart in cubes no bigger than dice.

We crossed stony creeks, we recrossed them, we drove along them for half a kilometre or so. A flood would remove all trace of much of the road. It was the wet season. There were storms in the distance. We called in to see Bob Clough at Epenarra. 'There's been no good rain for three years,' he said. 'I can't see the drought breaking in the next two days.' A waterhole in the Frew River at the back of his house had dried up. It is usually ten kilometres long. The oldest hands reckoned it was permanent.

Bob gets his mail and supplies by weekly plane, one can talk to him over the Flying Doctor network. Tennant Creek, the nearest town, is 200 kilometres away. The eastern boundary of the property is not fenced. In good years the cattle follow the magnificent feed on the Frew River floodout or down the many creeks that run from the west. He has to track them so that he knows where they are all the time or else they might get trapped on ephemeral claypan waters 100 kilometres away.

We crossed Hatches Creek and came to a sign PRIVATE PROPERTY NO ENTRY APPLY TO OFFICE. It looked as though it had been painted last week. There had been no one on the site except for a few fossickers for over thirty years. There are men's quarters still in fair order, several unroofed buildings, a high poppet head with massive cables still connected to the drums that worked them. Wolfram Hill, showing white quartz among the red rocks, dominates the area. It is now a waste of wild donkeys. Several watched us pitch camp, lovely animals. They are particularly big and in superb condition. They can maintain it on feed where cattle die. All show the dark shoulder stripe that records Mary's saddle.

We felt remote. Thunder and a few drops of rain clanging on the tent unsettled us. Even with the relic evidence it was difficult to people the country. I could not see Hector Mahomet loading his camels with ten tonnes of ore to cross some frightening dry stages north-east to the railhead at Dajarra in Queensland, or Charlie Sadadeen loading 400 to 450 kilograms each on a big string of strong camels for Oodnadatta, 1000 kilometres away on the South Australian terminus of the old line.

During 1942 and 1943 several hundred people worked there. They had a hospital, post office, police station, store, an air service, graded roads. The Chinese built comfortable huts roofed with galvanised iron and walled with hessian. They dug a cool meat room into the side of a hill, made an excellent garden, and selected the best mine props to make furniture. They compensated for underpayment and high-handed treatment by doing very little productive work.

So the government made nothing out of its mining venture. In November 1943 they closed down suddenly. Against a list of bracketed Chinese names in a timebook there is a notation: 'All joined the U.S.A. Army'. It is most unlikely the Chinese knew that. Every paper concerning them is marked SECRET. They were put aboard a convoy of trucks and sent to Brisbane to work in shipyards recently taken over by the Americans.

The next day the local police burnt their huts and destroyed the garden. The authorities could pretend they had never been there.

Cloud shadows
fall over them like
lengths of black velvet

No building in Alice Springs exceeds three storeys. Ancient hills dominate. They chaperone the young town.

I did not know Alice Springs was so hilly. I had read of Ormiston Gorge, Haasts Bluff, Standley Chasm, and thought them isolated wonders. Instead, they are greater wonders among hundreds of kilometres of wonders extending east and west across north and south.

They are not the blue mountains outsiders know. According to the light and to distance they are mauve, pink, purple, red, brown, grey, green, yellow, silver, spotted, tabby, polished amber. Cloud shadows fall over them like lengths of black velvet. Smoothly pleated main ranges are balanced by outriggers of low, jagged hills.

When one is travelling down the Stuart Highway, northern outliers of the MacDonnell Ranges presage what is to come. Steep-sided hills covered with shrubs and spinifex are capped by a bare flat crust of a different rock one and a half metres thick. Was it laid on top as an afterthought or didn't the hills rise properly? It is difficult to believe that they are real.

The hills that enclose Alice Springs have the same structured look. Steep, greenish, gravelly slopes run up to granite walls three metres high. The hills end abruptly, then begin again just as suddenly, leaving gaps that are named for different people: Heavitree, Simpson, Jessie, Emily. One can see no natural reason for them and the roads leading through them give them an artificial air. Gangs of convicts might have cut them.

The Todd River divides the town. It usually flows with sand instead of water but big River Red Gums find enough moisture under it. Every few years water swirls over their roots and they make a burst of growth while they can. It is an extraordinary transition from Darwin to Alice Springs, and one that a traveller can make in no other country. In 1500 kilometres one drives out of a region where plants and animals thrive in excessive wet to one where they thrive in excessive dry.

We thrived at Larapinta Lodge, an especially pleasant motel with a big communal kitchen that no one else used as successfully as Elaine. The mauve and pink outside light is imaginatively reproduced in the furnishings. Mark MacDonald owns it. He came to Alice Springs a few years ago as a science teacher. Now he owns two motels in that city and another in Darwin. His managers make a better job of the day-to-day running, so he is leaving them in charge and going back to university.

Chris McDonnell manages Larapinta. He came to the town as a tourist. As they drove out of it, the bus driver said, 'Well, folks! You can wave goodbye to Alice Springs.' So he did not wave and he came back.

The hottest part of the summer has always been slack in the Centre. Since we were staying more than a week, we arranged an excellent deal. Few customers were expected. Chris sent most of the staff on holidays. Then, by such good practices as sending a bus to meet every incoming plane, he kept the motel full. So he himself had to make beds and vacuum carpets.

But tourists are realising that people who live in such places carry on their normal work no matter what the weather. Why not travel then? Overseas visitors especially are taking advantage of the cheaper rates at unfashionable times. While we were there a convoy of Italians came through in eighteen four-wheel drive Fiats that they had brought with them. They had unloaded at Perth, driven across the Nullarbor, then up from Adelaide. They were about to leave the bitumen and make proper use of their gears. And Germans arrived in a big bus that they, too, had brought by ship. The driver pulled a lever at the back and a concertinaed kitchen opened out. Refrigerators supplied

*We drove out through the well-kept stone ruins
of Hermannsburg Mission . . .*

cold drinks. Awnings pulled out all round it, including one that made a dining shelter.

After three and a half months doing only what we should be doing (though that was the joy work ought to be), Elaine and I took one day off as tourists. We drove out through the well-kept stone ruins of Hermannsburg Mission down to the Finke River and had a picnic lunch under a grove of Red Cabbage Palms. The young palms name the species. They are brick red till they grow to about sixty centimetres.

Those we sat under were sixteen metres tall. For fourteen metres the trunk is straight and strong, then the last two or three metres spiral up to the leaves. Light glittered on them but it did not reach us. There are less than 1000 of these palms along a short stretch of the river. There are no other native palms nearer than 1000 kilometres. They are the only representatives of their species in the world. We sat in privileged shade.

*. . . Bilbies lead a boom
and bust existence . . .*

At Alice Springs we saw three Bilbies. We stroked them. They were young, they were in a pen, but only a handful of living people black and white have seen Bilbies anywhere. Rick Southgate is breeding them at the Arid Zone Research Station for the World Wildlife Fund. He hopes to save the species which is in dangerously low numbers.

They were once plentiful over a wide area. A stockman writing from the Riverina in the 1880s said their burrows were so thick it was dangerous to ride a horse about. They were common until 1900 in open sandy country south of Narrabri that the Pilliga Forest has now taken over. Aborigines of central Australia used their showy black and white tails for decoration. Young men, conscious of their looks, wore tassels of up to twenty secured in their hair and hanging down their foreheads or else dangling from woven hair waistbands.

Like the native plague rat of central Australia, Bilbies lead a boom and bust existence, breeding up to great numbers then disappearing for years. But it was rabbits that eradicated them from southern Australia. They took over the Bilby burrows. Possums and bandicoots had found them good homes too, but they caused no worry. Rabbits monopolised the burrows, reduced the food supply. It took them a couple of years only to wipe out the Bilbies.

Two waves of rabbits moved out of South Australia right up into the Tanami Desert, the first between the late 1890s and early 1900s, the second in the 1920s and 1930s. These reduced the Bilbies there, but, more seriously, cessation of Aboriginal burning reduced the seeding of annual grasses. Bilbies eat a lot of grass seeds as well as some green shoots, fruit, bulbs, insects and small mammals. They seldom get water to drink.

Rick Southgate made long journeys through lonely country to find out where they still exist. There are some in the Tanami Desert, others isolated in the Channel Country of south-west Queensland, a few more in north-west Western Australia. They are confined to better pockets in semidesert.

One expects to find Thorny Devils and giant scorpions in such a prickly environment. A Bilby in those surroundings looks as delicate as a butterfly in a hot house. Extraordinarily gentle, they might hiss a little when picked up but they make no attempt to bite or scratch. Their fur is smoke-blue, long, silky and beautifully groomed. It shines. Their long, naked ears are translucent, every blood vessel showing as clearly as a red network sketched on parchment. The long tail is black for about half its length, then white. They flag it as they run with a bounding gait. Snouts are long and pointed, with tender, bare pink tips.

The breeding group are fed on dog biscuits and budgerigar seed. They thrive on it and the females average six young a year. One year's batch, released under apparently ideal conditions in Simpson Gap National Park, disappeared. Rick does not know whether they died or migrated. He will fit the next release with radio tracking equipment.

Persuaded by Dr Ken Johnson, who is in charge of the Conservation Commission of the Northern Territory at Alice Springs, Aborigines are again burning the areas of the Tanami Desert where Bilbies live in an attempt to build up the wild population naturally. The Bilbies move on to burnt areas as soon as they sprout green.

Aborigines caught all the Bilbies used in the breeding program, though few are now expert in digging out the strange burrows. They twist down from a single opening in a spiral two to three metres in diameter and often go 1.8 metres deep. If a white man tries to dig them out with a shovel the Bilby merely digs ahead. Purlpura Davies of the Pintubi Tribe digs them out with a tin coolamon. She can look at a burrow, say, 'Oh, yes! It turns this way. The Bilby will be about here.' Then she quickly scoops out dirt straight down through several loops until she comes to it.

One day she dug out more than Rick needed so she ate the last one. Well, she had done a lot of clever work to earn it. Who ate the last dodo?

Another animal from the Tanami that scientists are trying to save is the Mala or Rufous Hare-wallaby, once plentiful, now so few the species might be doomed. There is one in a pen near the Bilbies. Very active, very agile, very nervous, they have to be approached quietly. Even though we crept up to the pen, it saw us and leapt wildly against the netting. We dared not talk to it, though we longed to say, 'Don't do that! Don't do that! You are one of the last of your kind.' We crept away.

The year 1888 was the worst
in Australian–Chinese relations

On 18 February 1888 the *Northern Territory Times* carried this advertisement: 'WANTED A GUIDE TO THE MACDONNELL RUBY MINES FOR 500 CHINESE.' It caused consternation throughout the colonies. The South Australian government tried to work out where along the route they could legally collect ten pounds sterling a head poll tax. New South Wales and Queensland protested that it might be a ruse. What was to stop them walking on?

The year 1888 was the worst in Australian–Chinese relations. Years of agitation by anti-immigration societies that were against all immigrants had engendered specific anti-Chinese leagues that counselled 'working men should unite to put down Chinese labour in every form; they should refuse to buy articles made by them; to deal in shops in which goods were sold by them; to cease dining in places in which they served as waiters; and if they came against a Chinaman on the footpath it was their bounden duty to shove him off it'.

The advertisement was never repeated. There are no records of any applicants for the job. No numbers of Chinese moved south. Elaine and I drove out to where they might have walked to ruby fields that might not be there. David Lindsay reported them in 1886. A fine surveyor, he crossed the Hale River and Harts Range when exploring the country between the Telegraph Line and the Queensland border. He found payable mica but he was more enthusiastic about the rubies: they were in extraordinary quantities.

Alice Springs was then no more than a telegraph station, the country is on the edge of the Simpson Desert. Yet about 200 men rushed the field. Twenty-four companies were formed with names like Great Matrix Ruby Company or Pearsons Extended Ruby and Precious Stones Company.

But there are few records of what they did. Stories persist. The first miners employed Aborigines to shovel sand in dry creek beds and pick out the stones they found. The miners sorted them, washed them, classed many of them as rubies and sold them for high prices. Then big consignments were made. Afghan drivers loaded up strings of camels and headed for Oodnadatta. Word came through by telegraph that the supposed rubies were worthless garnets. They dumped the loads along the track. The miners moved back fifty kilometres to Arltunga where some of them had noted alluvial gold on their way to dig rubies. Lack of water gave the field a slow start. About forty persisted by digging their own wells until Henry Luce found good reef gold. Then the government provided wells and a battery. The field maintained about 400 men until the early 1900s.

In 1981 Peter Forrest, whom we stayed with in Darwin, made an excellent report on the relics at Arltunga for the National Trust in the Northern Territory. Now the site is an Historical Reserve administered. by the Conservation Commission. Two rangers live there. There are the remains of stone houses, offices, the battery, a well, the police station, gaol, cemeteries, assay shed, and mounds of dirt piled up by shovel and windlass. Peter reported, 'It is a remote goldfield in a harsh environment . . . the evidence remaining interprets lifestyles on a mining frontier . . . Arltunga is of outstanding significance.'

Seven Chinese came on to the field. Ching Ah Wu took up a reef claim and put through three crushings. The others established a garden. But there was so much agitation against them they soon moved away. Ah Hong came in 1903 and began another garden. The European miners petitioned against him although he was the only source of fresh vegetables. So he moved into Stuart, the new village that became Alice Springs, and made another garden. Then he loaded his dray with vegetables and drove out each week to the goldfields to sell them. He must have spent all his time on the road. The round trip was 250 kilometres. The diggers paid three times more for their vegetables than if they had allowed him to garden locally but they kept their minefield pure.

We drove up a rough track to see White Range, the site of the early reef mines. White quartz dominates red quartzite. In a cemetery on the low slopes the finders of the two fields are buried, Joseph Hele who found the alluvial gold and Henry Luce. They are remembered by hand-hewn slabs of timber. Neither lived long. Since they died before Ah Hong began his rounds perhaps they died of lack of fresh vegetables.

I walked past the cemetery into the hills. It was easy to imagine myself distant. I looked to the north. Less than two kilometres away is a substantial mine. Bluey Bruce, after years of prospecting, has found the rich vein hundreds of others searched for during a hundred years. The road to his mine does not yet show on maps.

Near the entrance to the reserve there is a new hotel to cater for tourists. Sometimes the owner is a publican, mostly he is a miner. So was the first publican who set up on the same site about eighty years ago.

*Whatever gems
are up there are guarded
by flames*

Elaine and I drove on east past Arltunga along a washed-out, four-wheel drive track. We crossed a loop of the Hale River and camped beside it when we came to it again. The next day I walked twenty kilometres up it in a temperature that must have been well over 50°C. I am used to heat. I have never before been aware that the sun was close. It did not enervate me but it made me feel fragile. If my hat blew off, would I live to catch it? There could be doubt. Whatever gems are up there are guarded by flames.

The Hale River and its tributary creeks store them under deep white sand glistening with mica. For years at a time no water flows down it, yet the gorges it has cut through the red mountains are more spectacular than the gorges of the Katherine River. Tourists can get to those easily. Drive out along a bitumen road and get in an aluminium barge. It carries one up through a series of astonishing cliffs. But one can see what cut them. One is aware of the energy of water. When we went up a few storms had lifted the wide river two metres. Big logs came down on the brown flood. The boatman dodged them. There was evidence of floods twenty-five metres above us. The Hale River looks inert.

But it is fed by an astonishing number of creeks. There are more creeks in the MacDonnell Ranges where the rainfall is 250 millimetres a year than there are in the tropic coast where the rainfall is ten times more. The soil, unused to rain, does not absorb it quickly. Run-off is fast. In the rare periods of heavy general rain, creek joins creek joins river. The Hale roars down its gorges tossing logs in the air. And all that wild water has nowhere to go. It spreads into the Simpson Desert ninety kilometres away.

Perhaps every ten years the Todd River comes down at the same time. Their flood plains join and irrigate hundreds of square kilometres of hot bare sand. Dense green native spinach grows eight centimetres high in three days, eighty centimetres in a fortnight. Fleshy parakeelya throws up big, mauve flowers and daisies bloom yellow, yellow, yellow as far as one can see. The annuals shrivel in six weeks. The sand rebuilds its nutrients.

As one walks up the Hale River, the opaque orange-brown cliff faces of Ruby Gap become lighter in colour till at Glen Annie Gorge the faces are translucent amber, with patches of pink and crimson. From the river and the faces of this gorge, the first ruby hunters made their disappointing hauls. Beyond this gorge where the river widens, there is a patch of water-worn stones. They glint, they sparkle, they roll with colour. Individual stones present themselves. One might be walking over spilled chests of treasure.

Nearly all these stones are based on aluminium. So is garnet, so are rubies. The garnet from here is superior and nearer to rubies than ordinary garnet. Sometimes it is called Australian Ruby. True rubies were found in Harts Range about fifty kilometres to the north about ten years ago but they were small and inferior. It seems impossible that somewhere among these cliffs of near rubies that there are not pockets of true rubies. No one has ever made a substantial search. I believe that when those early loads were dumped valuable rubies were thrown away.

Emeralds and beryl are also based on aluminium. The early miners of mica who worked to the east of Glen Annie George found that wherever mica cut out, beryl began. They chipped out slabs as long and thick as their forearms. Did they point to emeralds? No one looked.

On the way back I sat in the shade on a green bank near a rare waterhole. The cliff opposite, thirty metres high, half a kilometre long, hangs like a mural. Three hundred and twenty million years ago the ground heaved up over a big area. Huge slabs of rock slid on one another. Molten greenschist ran between them, acted as a lubricant, and the speed of the slide accelerated. When soft rock slammed against hard rock, it bent, curved, rolled into coils. In comparatively modern times the Hale River cut its path and sculptured the story. It still shows clearly. One can see the coils, the dents where they hit, the lines of greenschist.

I looked down. A Fire-tailed Skink was running through the grass. It was a tiny thing. The tail was no more than twenty millimetres long. Yet it was so bright and moving so fast it seemed to leave a trail behind it. I could look up, look down between millions of years of marvels.

*. . . there is no water,
no fuel, no food
for 300 kilometres*

We set out for home from Ruby Gap, but not straight home. We needed to go east and began by driving west for 160 kilometres. Our detailed maps showed interesting tracks leading up the Harts Range on to the Plenty Highway. But tracks are impermanent in that country and anyway, we had not been able to talk to the landowners whose country they ran through. Some refuse access. They have spent too many hours and driven too many hundreds of kilometres helping motorists who have got lost, got bogged in sand or mud, broken down, run out of petrol, food, water. Breaking down in some of those areas would be equivalent to breaking down in a deserted Newcastle with the nearest homestead in Sydney. One becomes a considerable nuisance to more than oneself.

We called into The Gardens, a property on the dirt road back to the Stuart Highway, and asked about a track that led up an old stock route to the Plenty. 'You can't miss it,' we were told. 'It is fourteen miles down. There's a set of cattle yards on the left and another set of old yards on the right where you turn off. You can't miss it.' Northern Territory distances are unreliable. Sometimes a man says miles when he means kilometres, sometimes he says kilometres when he means miles, sometimes he does not seem to mean any particular distance, he just gives a figure.

So we both kept watching expecting to see an obvious turn-off not too far down the road. We missed it. By the time we knew we had missed it, it was easier to drive out on to the Stuart Highway, north a few kilometres then east on to the Plenty Highway that begins as a bitumen road and gradually deteriorates into a potholed track.

We crossed the wide, dry, shallow, sanded-up bed of the Plenty River and pulled in to Jervois station for fuel, the only bowsers in the 1150 kilometres between Alice Springs and Boulia in Queensland the way we went. Our extra fuel tank would have got us all the way but left nothing in reserve for wrong turnings. Jervois would not make much profit out of fuel sales. About three vehicles a day use the road. No one uses it after rain. We crossed the dry Marshall River and several creeks, all of which empty into the Simpson Desert, and slept off the road under the stars in a patch of Gidgee free of prickly spinifex.

In Queensland a big notice warns that there is no water, no fuel, no food for 300 kilometres. There is no road either in places. One selects the smoothest way through ruts and rocks where wheel tracks 150 metres wide show how other drivers have sought a way.

An old wooden boat tied outlandishly to a tree on the bank of what looked like a dry gully told us that we had come to the Georgina Channels and we were glad to cross them. Warm rain was travelling down from the tropic north, cold rain up from the antarctic south. If they met and multiplied the Georgina could come down thirty kilometres wide and close the road for weeks.

East of Boulia, when we were only hours ahead of the rain that closed the road for a week or so but did not fill the channels, the country was still very hot and very dry. Fall-offs from the MacDonnell Ranges stretched, floated, wavered, disappeared in mirage. We could not see what was real, what was image, how much was hidden. Seemingly solid hills disappeared into grey-blue shimmers, shimmers solidified into hills. The horizon floated.

We crossed the Diamintina Channels and came through Winton to Longreach, named for the big waterhole on the long reach of the Thomson River where Harry Redford (Captain Starlight of Rolf Boldrewood's *Robbery Under Arms*) put his 1000 head of stolen cattle together.

There we saw Chinese stonework at its best. Tim Hanrick showed us the overshot dam on Talleyrand. In the late 1880s gangs of Chinese miners who had not earned enough to go home worked

We are back in familiar country

in western Queensland. They put down ground tanks of 10,000 cubic metre capacity with pick, shovel, wheelbarrows and carry baskets. Then they carted stones in drays a distance of twenty kilometres and dammed creeks and gullies to fill them. The stones were not laid as a wall but as wide pavements with upright flat stones sloping with the current. They filled the interstices with pebbles. After a hundred years the dams still function. No stones have moved.

We came home through the Pilliga Forest. When I saw a bird I could name it, or a tree, or a flower. We are back in familiar country.

*. . . we unpacked the vehicle
after four months away
and 18,000 kilometres
of driving . . .*

John Hay, who took us into the Palmer River, looked at the electric winch on the front of our Toyota Landcruiser and said, 'That won't be any good where we're going. It won't work when you're upside down.' The winch favoured by those who drive in very rough country is a simple low-geared hand winch that works in water, or out of water with a vehicle in any position. And it has the great advantage of being much cheaper, much lighter in weight and much smaller. We found an unexpected disadvantage of our big winch. It cuts down air flow to the radiator and when the temperature gets over 40°C the normally cool-running engine begins to overheat, especially with the air-conditioner going.

As we unpacked the vehicle after four months away and 18,000 kilometres of driving, we considered how we will equip it for the next trip. We found tropic Australia so enthralling we are going back when the Chinese book is finished.

The basic vehicle is right, a diesel truck-type Toyota Landcruiser. There are virtually no other work vehicles in northern Australia and one can get spares anywhere. The station wagon type is not suitable. The vehicle is too long for sharp gully crossings, too heavy for bogs. The locals sneer at them as Hollywood vehicles.

So we needed a canopy and ordered one from a firm out of Newcastle that makes aluminium tippers for semitrailers. 'Cash only,' said the manager. 'I don't like carrying that much money about with me. Won't a bank cheque do?' 'Cash only,' said the manager. 'Do those who order a $6000 job pay you in cash? They'd have every pocket stuffed full.' 'Some of them bring it in suitcases,' said the manager.

He built us an excellent canopy but three weeks before we were to leave we decided that it would be exasperating crawling from the lift-up back door over tent, bedroll, folding table, drums of water, books, to get out something loaded in the front, that it was difficult to site the refrigerator so we could lift its lid up, that some of the country we were going into was so rough we would knock the windows out of the sides. John Britton in Coonabarabran built us another low canopy in two sections with a lift-up door over the refrigerator. We could reach everything from outside the vehicle and the solid sides stood up to knocking overhanging limbs out of the way.

Engel refrigerators are superb, they work off 240 volts AC as well as 12 volts DC, so is our little quiet-running Honda generator that kept the refrigerator running on 240 volts while it charged its battery on 12 volts. To fuel the generator we carried a drum of lead-free petrol which has more problems than the environmentalists who demanded it ever foresaw. It boils at 30°C so when the temperature reaches 40°C and over, as it does in so much of Queensland and the Northern Territory, service stations often cannot supply it. Their pumps will not handle the boiling, gassy liquid. Fill a metal jerry can more than two-thirds full and stand it in the open rack built for it and it puffs up into a lopsided sphere, as dangerous as a bomb to handle. It needs an insulated box.

Shovel, axe and mattock are essentials. Where does one carry them? I put them in the bottom of our trailer, each in a heavy jute sack, and piled things on top of them. They jiggled about like live things, cut their way out of covers and crawled under the spare wheels. Perhaps axe and mattock should be fitted to the bonnet where the army carries them. Shovel will fit under the table top somewhere, along with a spare spring, and a length of pipe to extend the wheel brace.

We fitted the biggest CB radio we could buy but its range is insufficient for remote country. When we went out into the South Australian deserts in 1966 we carried a powerful transmitter-receiver and crystals that allowed us to operate on the Flying Doctor network. Foolishly I allowed my licence to lapse. I have to apply for another. That is the only sort of radio suitable.

An extra fuel tank is vital (several times we travelled 900 kilometres between service stations). Those on sale are imperfect. Old pumps that cause diesel to froth, fast pumps for the huge tanks on road trains cause airlocks in them. An apparently full tank might be dangerously half empty. We had to keep a record of every litre of fuel we put in ours and of every litre we used. 'You should get forty litres of fuel in there,' I said to a girl at one service station. I undid the cap, letting built-up gas escape. 'Fill it slowly.' I peered down the pipe to see if I could see any fuel. It gurgled. It belched a litre of fuel all over me. Then it accepted that one litre only.

Everything on it knows its place

*Empty blocks
of lined A4 paper stand
in one right-hand corner,
waiting for words . . .*

I am back at my desk. It is not a proper desk, it is an old Silky Oak table that Joan and our elder son, Kim, bought at a sale somewhere shortly after we moved to Baradine eighteen years ago. One leg was loose so they glued and screwed it, they puttied up a wide crack down the middle. And how many hours have I sat at it since, ten to twelve a day, seven days a week for months at a time? It is still rock steady. I will not replace it if the Chinese book sells 100,000. Everything on it knows its place. Words come to it that I am not expecting.

Immediately to my left is a pile of handwritten notebooks that apply to the chapter I am writing. Some of them that I took to China were made for me by a conservator out of de-acidified paper. The paper will still be bright and sound 200 years from now. But alas, the ink will have faded. The permanent black ink I use is less permanent than the paper.

In the left-hand corner within frequent reach are eleven dictionaries and books of words. The Oxford is there and the Macquarie. There are marked differences in them and I accept as authority whichever one I agree with.

And there are *Brewer's Dictionary of Phrase and Fable* and Fowler's quirky *Modern English Usage* among Cantonese grammars and three Mandarin dictionaries which give old complicated characters and modern simplified characters, and Wade-Giles and Pinyin transcriptions which are different attempts at portraying sound. It took me two hours to find the meaning of a character last year, now I can look up the most difficult in two minutes. The new facsimile machines will simplify the sending of Chinese telegrams. Since the shape of characters could not previously be transmitted, each character was given a number, and a Chinese telegram consisted of a series of numbers to be looked up in the dictionary. Sadly, the astounding skills of some of the Chinese postal clerks will now be made obsolete. One man in Beijing knew the numbers of 10,000 characters.

Immediately in front of me is a typed outline of the book, its skeleton, and on top of it the pages of recent writing that I add to at the rate of five a day. Empty blocks of lined A4 paper stand in one right-hand corner, waiting for words to justify them and in the other, beyond the two fountain pens that have written all my books, and felt pens for correcting and scissors, glue, post-it pads, there is a disconcerting pile of letters that need answering. I love getting them and I try to answer them all between chapters but sometimes there are so many it is impossible. Some requests for information take a day or two to satisfy. Somewhere under the pile, I hate to think of it, there is a big brown envelope stuffed full of letters. It is marked with a black felt pen 'LETTERS THAT NEED ANSWERING BEFORE TOO LONG'. It is dated, how time flies, November 1985. Too many people altogether have been disappointed for too long.

A fruit tin that Kerry covered for me as a child holds spare pens, a big splinter of fragrant sandalwood from the Palmer River, a tail feather from a Swamp Pheasant, a silver skewer that Kim brought back from England (I use it as a letter opener) and a big female grasshopper with a male on her back that a Chinese on a Hong Kong corner folded miraculously quickly out of one long blade of rush-like grass.

Little soapstone turtles carved in China watch me from under papers. They signify long life so I gave them to Joan to carry in her purse when she was dying. Once she took them out and looked at them. 'They are not doing their job,' she said. 'I thought perhaps I'd knocked their heads off.' As paperweights there are a branding iron without a handle and two blocks of Mulga that a girl gave me about forty years ago. They cost her all my interest. Mulga was then kitsch with a capital K. Deplorable things are still being done with that timber but those two blocks now look beautiful.

Two weights I use with great care. One is a pair of silver hands on a lovely slab of white honeycombed rock. They remember that *The River* won Braille Book of the Year in 1975. The other is a perspex slab with a miniature cover of *A Million Wild Acres* buried in it, recording that the book was Talking Book of the Year in 1982. I am proud of those prizes. I have always said that I write to make people see.

*Field mushrooms
are a fruiting
of the very soil*

A crop of mushrooms came up to greet us after good rains not long after we got home. Elaine and I went out with buckets to pick them. Field mushrooms are a fruiting of the very soil. They present its smell and taste in exquisite refinement. Only a brown stain on the fingers records their origin.

It is several years since there has been such a big crop here but the mycelium they grow from has extended in that time. It works out in rings from a central point counting years like the growth rings of a tree. Many of the mushrooms were spaced about thirty centimetres apart around the circumferences of perfect circles up to four metres in diameter.

Some species of fungi produce nitrogen underground before they fruit and dark green rings show up in pasture. The English call them fairy rings. There is a perfect one in Elaine's mother's lawn that slopes down to the Brisbane River. A species of long-stemmed mushroom comes up sometimes to show that there are almost invisible white threads creeping underground, not fairies dancing at night about an insubstantial maypole.

Field mushrooms have a delicacy of flavour missing in cultivated mushrooms. So whether it be months or years that we wait between crops, we honour them with our best recipes. Joan made a Chinese soup with them so good we all made sure we had a copy before she died. It is one of the few Chinese dishes that fit European food and good wine. She sliced three lamb kidneys very thinly, mixed them with a teaspoon of cornflour and a dessertspoon of soy sauce, then fried them with about 200 grams of sliced mushrooms in just sufficient oil to cover the bottom of the pan. After three minutes when all was cooked, she added half a litre of hot water with an extra dash to make it up to the old pint, then simmered it for no more than ten minutes. The recipe recommended stock, not hot water, but that made this rich soup impossibly rich. It tastes its best if kept for a day or two, as most soups do. It is a black soup and attracts attention because it looks so different. It accents a white bowl and a silver spoon. One respects it before one tastes it.

Elaine picks out the big mushrooms and breaks off their stalks. She chops up the stalks, chops up chicken livers, a few shallots and parsley, fries them all in butter then stuffs the mushrooms with the mixture. She bakes them in butter and a little stock. Served as an entree they are so good it is difficult to find a course fit to follow them.

I fry mushrooms in butter for breakfast, put them on a thick piece of dry toast, then pour a sauce of hot cream and mashed anchovies over them. Essence of sea flavours essence of the soil.

One supreme recipe that I have been making for thirty years is no more than chicken, port wine and mushrooms. I cook them slowly in a heavy, enamelled cast-iron casserole and the three ingredients blend into a new bird.

Other species of fungi grow here that might be edible, might even be delicious, such as the white, fleshy puffballs that come up thickly. But there are big puffballs that grow in the forest that smell good and could be cut into thick white steaks. Are they the same species? I am not sure that anyone knows. Many Australian fungi have never been named. There are poisonous white earth balls that could be confused with puffballs so we do not risk eating any of them. Nor do we eat the white mushrooms that grow at different times from the field mushrooms. The few little books on fungi class them as especially palatable. But one bite of the imported white amanita now growing in Victoria is certain death.

Ink caps come up in thick masses along the decaying roots of a Kurrajong stump in the lawn. For a day or so they are delicate, folded, creamy-amber parasols, then the bottom edges decay and they drip back into the soil as black ink. They are edible when young if one does not drink wine, or any alcohol, twelve hours before or twelve hours after eating them. I refuse to watch the clock so closely.

Chinese herbalists sell a long-stemmed dried mushroom at enormous price. 'It's good for the blood,' they say. 'It comes from one mountain in the west and springs up as a tigress feeds her cubs. Where the frothy milk spatters from their lips to the ground, these mushrooms grow.'

They ought to be good for the whole body: essence of tiger from a wild mountain surging through the veins.

Life on the land
is good for all ages.
But it is especially good
for children

It must have been Easter Sunday 1965 when I gave rides to ten children who had not ridden before on Mitchell's Shetland pony, Beetle. He was nine hands high and had come down a year before from Tenterfield by train in a big box. He had been well mouthed but had never had a saddle on him. I did not know that till I approached him with a blanket. He reared and struck it out of my hand so quickly it was on the ground before I realised he had moved. So I talked to him. 'I'm not going to hurt you, Beetle. It's only a cloth. Here, smell it!' So he smelt it and accepted it and in a few more minutes accepted the saddle, too. In ten minutes, Mitchell, aged three, was on his back being led about.

He quickly learnt to walk, trot and canter to called orders and to work on a long lunging rein. So when I took children for rides I could stop running beside him now and then and let him circle while I had a rest. But children like to go somewhere when they are riding, so I spent most of the time beside him anyway.

We had a very long day that Sunday. Everybody wanted ride after ride. Beetle behaved perfectly. He allowed his ears to be fondled, his tail plaited. He was stroked, patted, prodded. Children unexpectedly jumped off on the wrong side. He never even flinched, or flattened his ears to say, 'That's enough!' When one little girl fell off and rolled under him he stopped, pivoted on one leg and put the others down as lightly as a ballet-dancer. When all were gone I led him back towards his yard. We passed the milking cow. Beetle jerked away, galloped round the cow in a tight circle, wheeled, buried both his back hooves deep in her belly, then trotted back to me and put his head under my arm.

Elaine and I spent last Easter Sunday at Tipari, the home of my daughter, Kerry Jane, and her husband, John Rich. It was Nicola's sixth birthday. She is their elder daughter. And Hamish was there, a fortnight old and beautiful, the first grandson despite my prediction that Kim and Sarah would have another daughter. Emma, their daughter, only just two years old, spent her day between the bookshelves and play with the other children. As they pulled up at the boundary gate, she said, 'They'll have different books on the shelves here, won't they, Mummy?'

Nicola and Philippa, her sister, have spent hours in bookshops since they were very young. They sit on the floor and turn pages with gentle assurance till they find a book they want. I have heard parents forbid children to touch books in a shop. 'Don't! You'll get it dirty!' Those children will never learn what it is to feel real words, thoughts made concrete. They will associate books, not with the complicated texture of living, but with ascetic, smooth white pages.

On Nicola's birthday card I brushed the characters for the nearest sound I could get to her name in Mandarin, Ní ge lǎ. The characters I used meant rainbow songs. If I had used other characters, the same sound would have meant muddy goose. Chinese have wonderful fun with European names. The tonal language allows endless punning. Although the austere Communists have tried to clean up the naturally bawdy language, Chinese, when they can get away with it, still select the dirtiest transliteration they can find for names of Europeans.

There were visiting children, too, and children of friends staying there. They played games to music, ran egg-and-spoon races, bowled brightly painted hard-boiled eggs that Amy, a beagle, and Fabian, a cocker spaniel, cleaned up as soon as they broke. Then Kerry caught Caroline, a mare she bought for her children, and gave them all rides. Caroline is a gentle old mare who can adjust her gait to capabilities, though, at seventeen she can no longer adjust to too much experience. Nicola

Life on the land . . .
is especially good for children

and Philippa will soon need more adventurous ponies. Then they can explore the forest next to them.

Kerry and Kim learnt on a mare named Old Creamy. She was twenty-seven so she had probably borne the Old additive for half her life. She was capable of little more than giving them balance and the feel of a horse. We kept her for three months only, then sold her to one of the list of people waiting for her. Creamy had spent her life teaching children to ride. People in their thirties remembered their first riding lessons on her.

In no time our children did all the stock work on the farm. We timed it for weekends or after school. From the time they were five they could help a ewe in lambing trouble. Their small hands fitted in much easier than mine to find out how legs were caught.

Life on the land is good for all ages. But it is especially good for children. It gives the experience to judge all things by.

It was a farming lifetime up for auction

T he clearing sale began as always on the back of a truck with tins of nuts and bolts, spanners, stilsons, pipe wrenches, chains, pulleys, fuel pumps, electric cable, drills and bits, fire extinguishers, soldering irons, bearings, rings, drenching runs, cultivator points, pipe fittings, a cast-iron glue pot from the last century. Small spaces had been left bare for the auctioneer and his offsiders to stand on. 'Sale Oh! Sale Oh! Sale Oh!' Bill Tapp, head of a firm of stock and station agents and well known in the district, addresses a circle of 300 to 400 people.

'We're selling account the Thurleigh Partnership, David and Harry Hadfield. We've got a lot to sell you today, ladies and gentlemen, all presented in immaculate order. I ask you to keep your bids coming in or the sale'll run so late you'll cut into our drinking time. Well, let's get on with it, what have we got?'

David Hadfield holds up a twelve tonne hydraulic jack. Young Larry Tolmie takes over. 'She's a goer that one,' he calls, 'lift all you want to lift, eighty dollars' worth there. Do I hear eighty, seventy, sixty, fifty, forty? Who's got twenty to give me a start? Twenty's the money, twenty-five, thirty I've got boys, over here, thirty's the money, thirty-five, forty called out the back, forty I've got now, forty, forty-five right here. Are you done? Out it goes. Done? Done! Number, sir?' And the penciller notes down the number on the card fixed on the buyer's hat brim, or pulled out of shirt or hip-pocket. He has registered his name before the sale began.

Larry calls so quickly it is difficult to take down what he says. There are no pauses. Like the old-time conjurors, he believes silence is death to the trick.

The next article is held up, sold, the next, sold. Soon Larry has room to move. Buyers stand with their purchases at their feet. The keenest seem to be growing out of them, a personification of odds and ends.

There is a slight hitch in the sale. One of the offsiders holds up a truck spring. 'It's the front spring for a Bedford,' explains David Hadfield, 'but I forget which model.' They bought it as a spare fifteen years ago, just before the old Bedford stopped work. They have had four or five old workhorses since. 'Well, it's a good bit of metal,' says Larry. 'Do I hear ten dollars, nine, eight, seven, six? Who's got a dollar to hear me go? Must be worth a dollar.' There is no bid. 'Well, put something else with it. What's in that tin? Hold it up, turn it round so everyone can see. Show those out the back. Five dollars I've got, boys. It'll go in one bold bid. Five dollars, done? Done? Done? Done.' He closes his hands half-heartedly. He did not have a bid. 'We'll have to start that one again, boys. Two dollars I've got over there. I've got it this time, two dollars. Done! Number seventy-four!' An auctioneer often has to work harder to sell something nondescript for two dollars than he has to sell a tractor for $20,000.

The sale progresses to bigger items laid out in rows in a mown paddock: wire netting, sheep feeding troughs, old tyres and rims, motorcycles, a wartime jeep with spare parts, old vehicles fitted up for fox-shooting, a vice on wheels for use in the paddock, welding gear, hammer mills, grain bins, then the big items of machinery: a bulldozer, grader, tractors, ploughs, combine, header, scarifier. All was presented in excellent order, all engines started at the turn of the key, though the sellers' stomachs tensed with each start. What if a trusty engine developed a nervous foible about the size of the audience? What if someone had fiddled with a connection somewhere?

All made good prices. Bill Tapp sold the big items, speaking slowly and holding buyers with voice, hands and eyes. He is a master. One can watch him pulling bids, hear him catch them. 'Twenty-six thousand, it is. It's against you, sir. Another thousand might wrap it up. What's another thousand?

. . . a farming lifetime up for auction . . .

It's only money.' His fingers reach out farther, eyes concentrate. 'Twenty-seven thousand!' Snap!

He uses humour to keep the crowd's attention through the seven tiring hours of the sale. 'I'll take hundred dollar lifts on this one,' he says, as he calls for bids on a farm truck. Five hundred dollar raises are usual on big machinery. 'I won't knock you up in raises of a Kings Cross night out.'

'Gawd! You'd knock up after twenty dollars' worth now, wouldn't you, Bill?'

A windmill was sold, still straddling the bore it pumped from when Harry and David were children. They have heard it knock as it changed stroke all their lives, watched the fluttering shadow of its blades on the ground.

'They must have had a bloody big row, those brothers, to be selling stuff as good as this,' someone said to me. But no, they are good friends. One wanted to retire, the other to farm less strenuously. They sold one of their properties, then the joint machinery.

It was a farming lifetime up for auction, forty-five years of hope and experience laid out in a final succession.

*The atmosphere of shows
is a wonder of vulgarity.
It is good to watch*

Several years ago during one of those periodic slumps on the land, it seemed that country shows would die. It was costing too much time and money to cultivate a district into a one-or-two day flowering. The opposite happened on the next bulge of optimism. One-day shows became two-day, two-day became three-day.

Elaine and I went to the show at Coonamble, one of our local towns. It is on the western plains. Only the Warrumbungle Mountains, vaguely pale blue about seventy kilometres away, show that the world is not flat black soil.

The grounds are on the banks of the Castlereagh River, and the water pumped from under its sands keeps them richly green with couch grass, whether naturalised or native no one knows. The buildings are of White Cypress Pine and corrugated, galvanised iron, materials that fit the Australian country better than any other.

The horses, the main exhibit, come in single floats, in double floats, in trucks old and new, in semitrailers fitted with lavishly appointed stalls. The horses vary in height from Shetlands of nine hands to Thoroughbreds of seventeen—horses wisely ignored the metric changeover. They all come in rugs, but the most valuable of them, especially those that have travelled long distances to join a new show circuit, are armoured against any possible rubbing or bruising. Tails are caught in canvas bags, extensions on the rug protect the upper part of the tails. Canvas gaiters are strapped on over-bandaged legs. Rubber guards flare down around hooves. Canvas shields protect heads, extensions on them cover manes.

*The buildings are of White Cypress Pine
and corrugated, galvanised iron . . .*

A horse that has travelled 400 kilometres has to enter the ring immaculate. Manes can be left to fall naturally but they have to be pulled so that every hair is the right length and no short pieces bristle up out of place. It takes constant hours. So most riders plait them, some with big plaits, some with many fine plaits, and that takes hours enough. Those horses got up in a hurry are likely to have their manes clipped, so are those ponies that have rolled in a patch of clover burr when given a run free of their trappings. Body coat has been washed, straw brushed, rough brushed, fine brushed till every hair glows in its best position. Tails have been drawn into shapely ornaments instead of careless appendages. Often the shorter hair across the fleshy upper part of the tails has been groomed into a length that permits a series of little plaits to be replaited into a ridge down the centre.

The riders live in caravans, tents, in cubicles on their trucks. Dress and equipment has to complement their horses. So all day there is washing drying on rope lines, clothes airing, coats being brushed, saddlery cleaned, boots polished. Queensland cattle dogs, Great Danes, German Shepherds, lying half asleep at the ends of their chains, leap to life if a stranger walks near.

Some of the riders are carried to their mounts so that no speck of dust mars even the soles of their boots. In the ring the riders control the great physical and nervous energy of the horses with aids that ought to be imperceptible. A slight shift of a toe, downward pressure on a leg causes a horse to change the leg it is leading by in a canter; an easing of the reins changes an ordinary trot into an extended trot. A horse does not stretch its front legs beyond its nose.

The riders make these moves with varying expertise, the horses respond according to training. When women rode side-saddle, a lady's hack had to lead naturally with its near front leg, otherwise the one-side load unbalanced it.

There were expert competitors in the timed jumping, a spectactular sport where jumps are scored according to the difficulty. The aim of the competitors is to make the highest score in sixty seconds. Well-trained horses show their enjoyment of jumping at speed. The even more spectacular high jumping has not been held for years. The record, I think, was something over two metres. Some riders adopted the extraordinary technique of jumping out of the saddle as the horse took off. As it cleared the top bar they would be half a metre clear of the saddle, then they settled back into place as the horse landed.

One can smell the lanolin in the wool pavilion before one gets to it. Black fleeces, once culled from flocks, now take their place beside the best white merino. Home spinners altered attitudes.

There are no longer Fowler jars packed with exquisitely home-preserved fruit in the cooking section, but chocolate-iced lamingtons mottled with desiccated coconut are still there, as well as sponge cakes and fruit cakes that judges strangely never taste. One wonders if the same cakes travel from show to show like so many of the horses.

Norman Turner displayed plaited whips that fall exactly where they are directed. He carves the handles of cowhorn or of many timbers: Yarran, Ironbark, Coolibah, Mulga, Gidgee, Budda, River Cooba, Beefwood, Bull Oak. Annette Rich presented embroidery as a living craft with a petticoat of astoundingly delicate work.

Fairy floss and toffee apples still sell as freely as they did fifty years ago. Waffles compete with them, chips, ice-creams of many thicknesses and colours and, surely now somewhat outdated, Dagwood dogs.

Plastic ducks move on endless belts through shooting galleries, a plastic frog hops into one of several bowls according to how hard a springboard is hit with a hammer, mini bikes and Shetland ponies offer rides side by side, merry-go-rounds that have not changed outwardly in 100 years run by electricity now instead of kerosene engines, the gravitron spins its riders dizzy among flashing lights and loud music.

The atmosphere of shows is a wonder of vulgarity. It is good to watch. People are acting with unconscious energy.

. . . thousands of grey
dead trees testifying
that water is death

This story could not be told before. Government departments were still making up their minds whether the project was permissible.

The Tinaroo Dam across the Barron River in north Queensland was completed under budget in the mid-1950s. Before the wall was finished, contract tree-fellers began to clear the valleys of timber. No timber was worth much then, it still seemed to be inexhaustible. The loggers planned to haul out the biggest of the good trees they cut down and leave the rest lying there. The dam builders were extraordinarily efficient: they finished well ahead of time, too. That did not worry the tree-fellers, who had not done much more than begin work. The dam was expected to take years to fill.

The cyclonic depressions that flooded so much of New South Wales in 1955 also flooded Queensland. Tinaroo filled in three days. Valleys of forest went under water.

Thirty years later Peter Mansfield, whom we stayed with at Atherton, realised the value of what was covered. He had seen it when diving. He formed the Kulara Timber Company, named for one of the submerged villages, to harvest it. They got permission to bring out a trial of 100 cubic metres. I saw logs of Red Cedar metres long and one and a half metres in diameter.

Many thousands of cubic metres of the finest and scarcest furniture woods are in the dam: Red Cedar, Queensland Maple (often known as Scented Maple) white, close-grained and prettily marked, Brown Salwood or *Acacia aulacocarpa*, dark red, tough and heavy, Queensland Kauri, light yellow and close-grained, and Black Bean, dark brown, figured, and usually hard to season. During thirty years the water seasoned it all superbly. Whatever is above the waterline has rotted, the fallen logs, the standing logs that have always been covered have absorbed silicon from the water. It preserved them and hardened them. Only saws with tungsten-tipped teeth will cut them.

I went out with Peter in a four-metre aluminium punt to bring in a particularly big log of Brown Salwood lying in about five metres of water just off the bank in one of the far reaches about ten kilometres away. We had an air compressor aboard, four empty sixty-litre drums, lengths of rope and a diving suit. We brushed over the dead brambly tops of trees in deep water, we passed between forked branches in the shallowest places. It is strange when one is told so often that water is life to have thousands of grey dead trees testifying that water is death.

On site we tied up to a dead sapling. Peter put on his diving suit. 'Where are your air tanks?' 'Don't bother with them,' said Peter. 'I suck on this.' He pulled a piece of rubber hose out of the coil attached to the air compressor.

What he sucked on was connected to the main hose by a pressure-reducing valve. He did not take his oxygen at 1400 kilopascals. The air also passed through a double filter so that he did not suck in too much oil and petrol. 'Don't worry about bubbles coming up,' said Peter. 'If they stop coming up, that's the time to worry.'

He let himself into the water. I handed him one of the empty drums and started the engine of the compressor. He unscrewed the bung from the drum and filled it with water so that he could wrestle it down alongside the log. He came back up for rope.

When he had tied the drums upside down in pairs at both the butt and the top of the log, Peter had to fill them with air. When he turned on the valve to feed the air up into the drums, he did not get any air through his feeder hose. So he held his breath for one minute, turned the valve off, sucked enough air to last him another minute, then turned it on again. His bubbles began coming up in spasmodic bursts.

*. . . grey dead trees testifying
that water is death*

And when the four drums were filled and the bungs screwed in place, the logs did not rise. Brown Salwood grew to an extraordinary size in that area. We came back for a 200 litre drum. When that was strapped on and filled with air, the log rose like a whale. It was hard, slow work for the 4.5 kilowatt outboard to tow it back. The punt lifted its bow as though it was planing. Much water had to be covered to find passages clear enough to get through. A tractor hauled the log out of the water and up to the dump. Peter brought in most of the experimental logs on his own, dangerous work with such primitive gear.

Now they are building a big aluminium punt equipped with a hoist to lift the logs. One of the company directors built a waterproof electric chainsaw so they will also install a generator on board. They will use complete diving gear. It will be relatively easy bringing in the sawn logs with the new equipment, but under the terms of the licence they have to clear big areas of the dam for boating. Hundreds of trees have to be cut off at the butts in water up to twelve metres deep. It will be dangerous work. How does a tree fall under water? Those not fit for timber will be piled on the bank and burnt when they dry.

In a year or two Australian craftsmen will work some of the best timber ever marketed.

*Our past is still very near
and it was often very savage*

Elaine has a new job. She noticed an advertisement calling for field officers for the Australian Bicentennial Historic Records Search. She knows a lot of history, she loves dealing with people. In Brisbane under the umbrella of Blocksidge and Ferguson, a century old company of agents and auctioneers, she matched the sellers of architecturally and historically important houses with buyers who knew how to manage them. We drove to Tamworth for an interview.

What would you do if you broke down on a back road on the way to an important meeting? Her area stretches from Walcha to Wanaaring, from Binnaway to the Queensland border. It is almost a third of the state. The organisers needed to know if she could cope with lonely blacksoil roads.

If somebody rings you and tells you they have a collection of postcards sent from the Gold Coast between 1950 and 1970, would they be worth looking at? That was the question that distinguished the officers they wanted from historians and archivists. The academics concentrated only on the front of the cards. Did they show important changes in building, in landscape? Elaine turned the cards over and read them as well. The people might be known, she said, but above all, that period ought to document social change. Those cards could be valuable.

Cathy Santamaria first had the idea of the search. She was manuscripts librarian at the National Library and had seen the historic manuscripts register in London. The English interest was in important people only. Stephen Foster and Peter Spearritt, unacademic academic historians, took up the idea from Cathy. They considered that the most important documents in Australia would be in the hands of ordinary people. The field officers would turn up history that had never been recorded.

Word had to be got out somehow. Blue's Country Mail Bag covers the area, a plastic envelope with a blue heeler imprinted on it, full of advertising pamphlets and a memorandum from Blue, Sniffin' About. Elaine stamped 9000 description sheets with her name, address and telephone number. Blue consigned them. She expected 400 replies within days. She got three or four. She did radio and television interviews; two or three proferred records. Country people respond with caution. Many had the idea that their records might be confiscated. Their distrust of government is not without foundation. One woman at Wee Waa who had kept ninety years of flood records that proved a government department wrong in many of their statements, did have her most embarrassing records stolen by a smart young man sent up to copy them.

So Elaine put an answering machine on the telephone in her Tamworth office, took off her skirt and street shoes, put on jeans and riding boots, left me her Corolla, and headed west in the Landcruiser utility equipped with the winch and long-range fuel tanks that we put on for our trip north. She looked part of the country and people responded to her warmth.

What she had to do, what she will evidently have to keep doing, is work through historical societies, through people we know, through people we know of. One family leads to another. It is a matter of going to a town, seeing people, telephoning people in the hope that word and trust will spread.

She was shown photographs of paddle-wheel steamers on the Barwon, then taken out and shown the heavy rope still dangling from the tree that moored them a hundred years ago. But the river has cut a new path in that time and the rope now waits for riverboats over a wide, dry gully. The wife of one family was enthusiastic about having their papers catalogued; Elaine was anxious to see them, they went back to the 1830s. The visit was revoked when the husband got home. The papers concerned his family and there were more skeletons than usual hidden among them. Our past is still very near and it was often very savage.

Elaine came home from her second trip excited by what she had found at the home of Len Cram in Lightning Ridge. He is a fine photographer, he has a supreme knowledge of opal. His slides of stones in the rough and polished number thousands. Jewellers throughout the world draw on them for advertising.

But he also realised the importance of the diggers at work, and since the 1950s he has made a record of most Australian fields on still and moving film. He photographed the Hayricks Field of milky boulder opal out of Quilpie, Queensland, when genuine miners were working it. A greedy company moved in with bulldozers and destroyed it all. They harvested some opal, smashed most of it.

Even on Len Cram's early black and white eight-millimetre film, the opal seems to flash. It lives on his coloured video tapes. His photographs are important to the records search, his film is outside its sphere. Elaine notified the National Film and Sound Archive of the extraordinary holding.

An incidental box contained hundreds of negatives of Taree in the 1920s, each in an envelope with the name of the professional photographer who took them. 'What can I do with them?' asked Len. Realising their importance he had rescued them from someone somewhere who was taking them to a tip, but he wished to renounce responsibility.

Elaine knew that Taree is building an Historical Resources Centre that will have the facilities to preserve them. Such linking of source and location will become an important part of the search.

There are thirty field officers at work throughout Australia, chosen from over 600 applicants. When they have all finished work in a year's time their findings will be compiled at the National Library and distributed on microfiche to all Australian libraries. Our white history should have grown extraordinarily.

*A facsimile window
loses its original rattles,
the arms of those
who opened it*

We spent a week in Sydney staying with one of Elaine's tall sons, Adam, in the Shipwrights Arms in Windmill Street, built as a home in 1831, then turned into a public house. The exterior walls are of handmade bricks, the interior, still in good condition, is a plaster of sand, lime and cow hair over narrow, spaced laths. George Paton, a stonemason, bought that part of the land extending into Lower Fort Street in 1843 and built The Hero of Waterloo from the blocks of sandstone taken out of the Argyle Cut. By then Jonathan Clarke, owner of the house, had gone out of business. Paton opened as a publican in 1845.

And his building is still a thriving hotel. The bare, sparrow-pecked stone inside shows the individuality of the masons. Some decorated them with broad picks, some with narrow picks, with strokes of different length, of different spacing, of varying angles. A long tunnel is still in place leading from the cellars to the water. During the 1850s when captains were desperate to replace those sailors who had jumped ship for the goldfields, unwary drinkers were handed a Mickey Finn, dropped through a trapdoor, and carried down the tunnel to a waiting rowing boat. They woke as seamen on a ship already at sea.

These remarkable buildings are part of a group saved by Jack Mundey from developers and a crooked government in the 1960s. The Maritime Services Board is now the owner in a complicated arrangement. It has done some recent bad renovating, replacing the old soft mortar between bricks with cement. This cut the flow of rising salt which used to exude harmlessly through the lime and sand. Now it forces its way through the bricks as the softer material, and blocks of them are crumbling.

The Shipwrights Arms was an appropriate house from which to walk up to the old Fort Street Girls' High School and hear Philip Venning speaking as a guest of the National Trust of Australia. He is the secretary for the Society for Protection of Ancient Buildings in Britain. This remarkable body was founded in 1877 by William Morris, poet, architect, printer, craftsman, novelist. He believed that old buildings do not belong to one generation. They belonged to forefathers, they will belong to descendants. One stone building in England, built early in the tenth century, is still a good house to live in.

Venning considered that Australia's slab huts and corrugated-iron sheds are important. They show how people lived and worked. Grand buildings are unrepresentative: the Hanging Gardens of Babylon instead of the mud rooms. Some of the best buildings in Britain were saved by a shortage of money. Nothing more could be done than protect them. Money brings the problem of people trying to restore things. A copy preserves only the idea of an object. A facsimile window loses its original rattles, the arms of those who opened it.

Adam van Kempen walks from the Shipwrights Arms to his job at the Argyle Tavern, a group of five restaurants. At eighteen he is bars manager. They cater mostly for American and Japanese tourists and it requires diplomacy when busloads of each come through different doors together. Some Americans consider they have precedence and insist on it raucously. They have to be refused in such a way that it does not mar their appetites.

We also went that week to the opening of the Charles Blackman exhibition at the Bonython–Meadmore Gallery. A recording of the opera, *The Magic Flute*, played in the background. Canvas and paper in Blackman's series of the same name swirled with colour instead of sound.

Elaine's daughter, Sue, had four big pieces of her ceramic sculpture on show there, too. She is fascinated by the play and interplay of light around tall buildings, by their shadows and reflections, by rays streaming down between them, by glints off glass, steel, brick and concrete. She takes photographs from angles that make the buildings themselves look like sculptures instead of constructions.

She works with big slabs of clay, forming them into cubes or rectangular boxes. The consistency of the clay is crucial and requires much experiment. Through a vent in what will be the bottom, she packs shredded paper to stop the sides sagging. It burns during the bisque firing at high heat in electric kilns, and the gases escape through the vent. The reddish boxes come out of the oven set firm like biscuit. She places one on the other in the form that she wants, then puts on paint and glaze to resemble splashes of light in places, to reflect light in others. Then she fixes the paint and runs the glaze with another firing. Clay and paint concentrate the atmosphere of many storeys.

I speak as I write,
deliberately,
deciding just how best
to say it

I put myself on show in *Sunday Afternoon* with Peter Ross on ABC Television. A couple of months ago, after an invitation to appear on the program, Elaine and I had morning tea with Cynthia Connolly at the Art Gallery. It is Cynthia's job to do the research: to find out what each guest speaks best about, to record accomplishments, interests, refusals of any subjects, and also, there is no doubt, to deduce what can best be done with the guest if, despite their careful initial investigations, she finds they have picked a dud.

We enjoyed meeting Cynthia and it was a delight for me to be talking and having someone else making notes. When I am not writing I am on research and it is usually I asking questions of someone and recording answers. We went out to the studios at Gore Hill for preliminary talks with Peter Ross and George Pugh, the producer of the program. These interviews are not the casual chats that Peter makes them appear on the screen. They are that way because of the work he does beforehand.

On the morning of the taping, a chauffeur-driven Mercedes picked us up at seven o'clock. Guests have to fit production schedules. Cynthia met us and guided us through the huge warren of buildings divided into rooms, cubicles, studios. Props are stacked against walls, shelves bear boxes of tapes marked with familiar names, some current, some out of production. The place is already alive with people, all seemingly urgent. The clocks are insatiable. They demand perpetual offerings of schedules timed to the minute.

I went to the make-up room. These used to be officiated over by girls displaying their art with long, false, red fingernails, intricate hairdos fixed in place with spray, and faces more iced with cosmetics than dusted. These days they are more likely to wear no make-up at all. They toss their natural hair back and get to work. It is mostly a matter of shading the shiny spots so that what the camera reproduces looks like skin not metal. They keep testing their mixes of colour. The camera exaggerates differences in tone and might see left hand a different colour from the right.

I enjoy talking to big audiences from a stage. I can walk about, wave my arms, speak to individuals or groups all around the hall. Before the camera I sat brightly lit in a chair facing Peter Ross. I was conscious of wires, machines, producers, technicians in the background but could not watch them or talk to them.

'Move your chair a little more round this way. Test it for squeaks. That's good. Now look in this direction. You can move your head through about that angle.'

One sits plugged into the machinery by the microphone fastened under the coat. A make-up man in jeans, sneakers and T-shirt gives us a final dusting. I watch Peter Ross, imagine an audience, key myself up. This is not my way of talking. I speak as I write, deliberately, deciding just how best to say it. On radio or televison there cannot be long pauses. One has to be instantly interesting.

'Ready, Antoine?' Peter asks the head cameraman.

'No, a minute yet . . . ! Thirty seconds . . . I've got a loose tooth, it might drop out.'

There is constant in-house banter, sometimes obscure.

'Break a leg everybody! Here we go!' Peter gives the traditional showman's blessing.

'Fifteen seconds, ten.' Peter clears his throat. The girl working the autocue moves her finger above the button. The screen begins to roll behind me. Peter introduces his program. He does not always bother about what is on the screen. Sometimes he had to ad lib anyway. For some unaccountable reason the autocue several times broke into nonsense.

He tapes the interviews in four seven-to-ten-minute segments that fit into a four-hour show of music, dancing and documentaries. He keeps the right questions coming. One can relax and talk. At the end of the first section I said involuntarily, 'You're good, Peter, there's no doubt!' During the intervals Cynthia sometimes reminded Peter of questions. She queried one introduction. 'Is it the Vienna Symphony or Vienna Philharmonic?' 'Symphony,' replied Peter. 'That's from the music department . . . Right! Are we happy to move on? Here we go! Stand by!'

I finished by talking about the joyful life Joan and I had led together and I said a poem, *Last Kiss*, that I wrote for her after her death. It is probably my best. Peter tried to close the program and could not. 'I'm sorry,' he said. 'That affected me. We'll have to wait.'

The cameraman filled in time with still shots of me to use if or wherever necessary. 'Don't speak now, just nod as if agreeing. All right! Now don't nod, just sit as if you are listening.'

The next day I taped a radio broadcast for the Canadian Broadcasting Company's science show, *Quirks and Quarks*. It was about the exceedingly complex result of the introduction of European animals and farming methods to a country as different as Australia. I had given them *They All Ran Wild* and *A Million Wild Acres* to read, plus published talks.

The interview was in a small bare room at the University of Sydney. I had to sit facing closely into a wall to get the sound right. I could not see the interviewer, who apparently had read nothing I sent him. He did not give me one helpful question. For forty-five minutes I had to answer fluently the questions I was not asked and somehow make it seem I was responding to what he did say. The sweat poured off me. They got a good interview. The subject is so fascinating I was determined to explain it properly.

I cannot even say they more than got their money's worth out of me. I was not being paid.

The district tractors have done their
twenty-four-hour-a-day stint . . .

*This house is secure
again with the love
that it always knew*

The crops are up. The district tractors have done their twenty-four-hour-a-day stint and the paddocks are green with lupins, wheat, barley, oats and triticale that grow so well here. Already the cereal crops have secured themselves with the permanent roots that flare from the seedling stem just under the surface of the ground. On the rich black soil that we farmed at Boggabri twenty years ago, there was always an anxious wait for the good rain to encourage these roots. Seedling roots lose their energy after seven weeks and the fluffy, self-mulching soil dried out on top so there had to be a good follow-up fall about a month after sowing. At Baradine, not only do light falls of rain soak much more deeply into the sandy loams, but there is more upward capillary action to keep the topsoil moist. Particles of black soil slide about on one another and keep rearranging the pore spacing. The soil is more stable here. Usually the sowing rain is sufficient to produce the permanent roots and the plants can survive an extra few weeks without rain if they have to.

This year, also, we have no crops sown, and perhaps I shall never again make use of the marvellous science of growing them. There are too many books that I have to grow to allow me to do the work directly and this farm that supported a family and a farmhand or two so well for so many years can no longer afford to pay wages. Rising costs demand more land, as they have always done. Two hundred years ago when men farmed with hoes and scythes, twenty hectares provided for them. Ironically, many of those who obeyed the dictum 'Get big or get out' several years ago borrowed too much at too high interest from eager lenders and found themselves ruined when prices of wheat, fat lambs and cattle dropped for two or three years. Farming, which is a long-term business, depends too much on short-term money.

But this year we are not fattening sheep either. Drought-breaking general rains brought such a rise in store stock, there is too little margin between buying and selling prices. John Johnston, a neighbour, took the farm on agistment. It enabled him to hold all his lamb drop for the expected rise in wool prices. He has just called in to say he found a bower that our Spotted Bowerbird has built.

I have looked for his display grounds often but until now he must have performed off the property. This one is complete but of fairly recent construction. He speared long grass stems into the ground and laced them together thickly into an arched hall about sixty centimetres long. He has not done any beak painting yet with charcoal or bruised berries but he has hung two aluminium ring pulls on one wall and a length of yellow twine on the other. About both entrances he strewed bleached vertebrae from a long-dead sheep, shrivelled creamy berries off the White Cedars and little green oranges. There is a broken yellow cattle ear tag and a few galvanised nuts. He must have been into somebody's shed.

He has kept up with changing times. None of these adornments were available to his ancestors of 200 years ago.

Unusually, this bower is hidden. It is under a spreading Giles Net Bush in a fenced off plantation. A female could not see it from the air. He must call them in to watch him parade with outstretched wings, to run through the arch, to hop back, to move his baubles about. If he does it with the right flair, perhaps she will mate with him.

I offer my books to Elaine. We intend to marry in a year or so. Why does marriage make any difference? Are we following old-fashioned prejudices? Neither of us explores our actions, neither of us is influenced much by outside opinions. It simply seems a good thing to do. The advertising

*The advertising of love by marriage
somehow deepens it*

of love by marriage somehow deepens it. This house is secure again with the love, the good sense, the rich living, the hard work that it always knew.

Our marriage will not be for making children. Both of us have already made them and they will be a vital part of the union. Elaine would not have interested me, I would not have interested Elaine without the extraordinary quality of our children to bolster us. Whatever a man or woman has done is incomplete without children to maintain the same excellence in their own different fields. Talent has to grow talent or it fails posterity.

Much of our future depends on *Flowers and the Wide Sea*, the book that is now growing each day. That is as it ought to be. A writer, like a farmer, has to risk himself.